Veronica Krestow

THE

VISIBLE

EMPATH

Clear Seven Core Visibility Blocks
& Confidently Voice Your Message That Moves the World

Printed and bound in the United States of America
ISBN: 979-8-9997950-0-7

Come home to calm confidence

Download your free *5A's* guided audio at thediamondprocess.com/
regulate and practice for 5 days in a row (5 A's for five days). It's a
nervous system reset that helps you feel safe being seen, speaking up,
and embodying true confidence being fully you.

Dedicated to the big-hearted souls—
the empaths, the feelers, the light bringers who fear being seen:
your light was made for these times.

You came for this ...

There's something you know
Something you knew way before you picked up this book
A song in your soul you came here to sing
A message you came here to serve, whether you know exactly
what it is or not
The frequency of love wants to burst through you, your life,
and your words
I believe it's part of why you came to our Earth
For this deep wisdom and inferno of love that fires from
within you
You've been through trials in your life
You've fallen
There were times you didn't think you'd get back up
But you did
And you did
Again and again
Because this Love inside you is unrelenting
She will not let you quit, because you were meant for this
You came for this
She tugs at your sleeve with visions of sharing your voice
She knows your soul
She knows you rose from the ashes like a phoenix
And that you're here to help others rise too

She knows how ancient the wisdom is that you carry
She also knows to hold you tenderly and guide you until you
strike joy
The joy that comes from turning off the bad news and
becoming the good news
The elation of owning your worth, your expertise, and
magnificence
The page has turned
It's time for you to stop absorbing the ways of the world
And confidently rise as a lighthouse
As the good news
Not by avoiding the dark, but by having the courage to
loyally shine within it
Everything supports you now
The book you're holding right now is an invitation into the arena
It's your time to shine!

Contents

Why I Wrote This Book

I t was one of those damp Northern California afternoons, where the sky hangs heavy and the fog drapes itself over the trees like a weighted blanket. As the first drops of rain began to fall, I ducked into a little brick-and-mortar shop tucked between two old buildings. The moment I stepped inside, the atmosphere wrapped around me like a cashmere pashmina—warm, grounding, and instantly leading me to audibly exhale.

I paused at the entrance as I took in the space. A golden glow radiated from curated lighting. The air carried the scent of hand-poured soy candles, some embedded with tiny quartz crystals. Shelves held handmade blankets, bath bombs, and self-love oil blends that felt more like rituals than products. Sound healing instruments stood like gentle guardians, humming with intention. Behind the counter was a woman with kind eyes and a welcoming smile—the kind that makes you feel at home before a word is spoken.

We started talking, and before long she asked, "Where do you live?"

"Portugal," I said.

Her eyes widened. "That's amazing. What do you do that allows you to live in Portugal?"

I told her how I'd once quietly started a YouTube channel, sharing what was helping me heal emotionally and grow spiritually. I didn't tell anyone I knew because I was afraid of being judged. Who was I to share words of wisdom online when I was going through my own personal struggles? I continued to tell her how that small step evolved into a thriving business in which I now help empath entrepreneurs, coaches, and healers clear visibility blocks, confidently share their voices, and grow meaningful businesses. As I spoke, I could see something stirring in her.

"I can't believe you walked into my store and we're having this conversation right now," she said, her voice a little shaky. "I was just writing about this in my journal this morning." She glanced toward the door, then leaned in like someone revealing a secret. "I dream of moving to Mexico. I want to do healing work virtually … but I know I need to be visible to attract clients." Her voice dropped to a whisper. "And I'm terrified."

I nodded. I knew that fear well.

Visibility can feel like standing under a spotlight with your heart exposed. The fear of judgment, the vulnerability, the inner critic that screams, *Who are you to do this?*—it's a familiar storm. But what I've learned is this: Staying invisible doesn't serve our dreams, our purpose, or the people who need what we have to offer.

So I told her the truth.

And this book is an extension of that truth. It's my answer to her question: "Where do I start?"

Advance Praise for
The Visible Empath

"If you are someone who wants to more truthfully live in your intuition, your sensitivity, your empathy, your essence, and authentically lead from this place … this treasure of a book will help you dream your life and live your dreams. No phony promises. Just truth. Its author is one of the truest people I know. Learn from her."

—**Laura Munson**, *New York Times*, *USA Today*, and international best-selling author of *The Wild Why: Stories and Teachings to Uncover Your Wonder*, and founder of the acclaimed Haven Writing Retreats

"The *Visible Empath* is more than a book—it's a sacred transmission for sensitive souls who know they're here to make a difference, but have struggled to be seen. Veronica has given us a profound, practical, and deeply compassionate guide to reclaim our voice, visibility, and divine purpose. As someone who's walked this path myself, I felt understood, empowered, and called forward in these pages. This is a must-read for every heart-centered leader, healer, and empath who's ready to show up fully and shine from soul."

—**Julie Reisler**, Host, *You-est You®* Podcast, Author, TEDx Speaker, Intuitive Coach + Founder, Intuitive Life Designer® Coach Academy

"Veronica, I love the work you do! Keep shining and helping others shine!"

—**Kelly Gores**, Writer, Director, and Host of the award-winning *HEAL* documentary, author of the *HEAL* book, and host of the *HEAL with Kelly* Podcast

"Veronica is an original thinker who has birthed an amazing book. *The Visible Empath* is a much-needed handbook for the sensitive souls out there helping guide others to the light. This book will replace some of the old imagery about the wounded healer and replace it with newer language and exercises for the empath in all of us ready to be seen and heard! Read it, do the exercises, and set yourself free!"

—**David Elliott**, Author of *The Reluctant Healer, HEALING* and Founder of the Healer Training Breathwork program

"*The Visible Empath* offers invaluable wisdom from an extraordinary leader who embodies what it means to navigate the world with both sensitivity and strength. Veronica Krestow demonstrates that being an empath isn't about shrinking from the world, it's about engaging with it powerfully and authentically.

"Her guidance shows us that empathy can be a source of profound personal power when we learn to honor it rather than hide it. This book is essential reading for anyone seeking to embrace their empathic nature while maintaining their boundaries, their voice, and their impact. Veronica's words will resonate deeply and offer practical pathways for growth."

—**Hemalayaa,** Founder of Embody Costa Rica, Guide to Joyful and Embodied Living, and The Yoga and Indian Dance Fusion Pioneer

Who This Book Is For

If you're an empath, highly sensitive person, or coach who feels this burning clarity that you have a valuable message to share with more people, but you're afraid to step into the spotlight, you're not alone in this. Struggling with self-doubt, feelings of not being good enough, overthinking, imposter syndrome, perfectionism, people-pleasing, or anxiety that stops you in your tracks is something so many talented sensitive leaders face.

Maybe you're frustrated because you want to feel confident being visible so you can help others and make an impact, but your fears and doubts have you frozen in non-action. This yearning to be authentic and of service may be bubbling up from within you. Or, you might have a wealth of knowledge, valuable skills, and are already making a difference in people's lives, and you're called to share your deeper message with a wider audience. Maybe you even dream of being visible online so you can leave your current job, create a global community, and enjoy more freedom as you grow your business. You might imagine your dream life, working from anywhere on your own schedule. If you see yourself in any of this, I'm so happy you've picked up this book, because I wrote it for you!

Months ago, I started working with a new client, who confessed to me that being stuck in silence about her story and life lessons keeps her awake at night. Her eyes wide open in the dark room with her partner by her side who didn't have a clue about the struggle she was in for years. Years! She'd quietly stare up at the ceiling picturing herself on stage, empowering young moms who have lost their sense of self. The calling was so strong, but no matter how clearly she saw it, she wasn't able to act on it and even felt embarrassed by her dream. She'd shame herself, *Who am I to want this? People would think I'm ridiculous if they knew I wanted to speak publicly and help other moms. There's nothing special about me.* She'd always been a lifelong learner, but when it came to sharing what she knew, internal blocks kept her hiding under the covers—literally!

Fears of failing, being judged, not feeling good enough, and perfectionism kept preventing her from confidently sharing her expertise. She typecast herself in the silent student role, which was her comfort zone, and didn't allow herself to venture into expressing her unique wisdom. Still, this calling wouldn't let her go. She stumbled upon one of my YouTube videos, joined Confident Visibility School, and now she has her own YouTube channel and is growing her online community.

Like so many I work with, this woman is a lighthouse, and she wasn't willing to wait a moment longer to free herself and her valuable voice. All of those years resisting her dream were like the pulling back of an arrow on a bow. First, the bowstring is drawn back as far as it can go as you grit your teeth. Then, there's a point when you can't resist any further; your fingers release the string and the arrow flies forward. This is what happened with her. She resisted her dream until she gained so much tension that she stopped resisting, released, and sprang forward. All she needed was the safe container to let go and be seen, the tools to clear her visibility blocks, and the guidance to courageously start sharing her message in an effective, empowering way—all of which I'll be sharing with you in this book!

If you've been resisting being seen and sharing your valuable message, it's okay. This is part of the process. Now is a great time to let go of any judgments about it. Trust the timing of your journey and celebrate! It has brought you here.

Because I work mostly with women, my words are directed mainly to them, but the heart of this book is for anyone who longs to contribute their gifts and wisdom in a bigger way. No matter your age, gender, or orientation, if you've ever struggled with visibility fears, you'll find encouragement, practical tools, and transformation waiting for you in these pages.

Introduction

How to Use This Book

Self-trust is the first secret of success.
—Ralph Waldo Emerson

This book is designed to help you feel safe being seen and confidently voicing the message that lives within you over a 28-day transformational moon cycle. One complete moon cycle to phase into your full confidence and free your authentic voice. You can start on the full moon, representing your commitment to step into your full glow. You can start on the new moon to support your deepest intention of being confident and visible. Really, you can start anywhere in between the new and full moons, knowing that whatever day you choose to begin is the perfect day for you.

You can read this in 28 days or 28 years. There is no right or wrong way to receive the gems that this book has to offer you and your visibility. Although it's designed to be read over one moon cycle, you can take your time with it.

Each day is intentionally a short, digestible sliver of inspiration, holding an insight to help you step into confident visibility in a lasting way. At the end of each day's chapter, you'll see a video diary prompt. This a simple, yet transformative daily practice that I encourage you to commit to. You'll be amazed by what happens when you express your voice on video for your eyes only, as you would in a diary. In my courses and membership, I have seen student after student experience massive breakthroughs from video diaries alone.

One alternative way to use this book is to spontaneously flip to one of the chapters and let that be your lesson and video diary prompt for the day. However you choose to receive this empowering book is perfect for you. The key is to dive in and let the magic held in these pages unfold. Discover how your devotion to the visibility practices cultivates a deep sense of safety and confidence within you.

LOVE NOTE: Some of the video diary prompts and practices invite deeper exploration. Avoid exploring fresh, unhealed wounds while reading this book unless you're working with a certified therapist or trauma specialist. This book is not a replacement for professional therapy. It's important to meet yourself with safety, stability, and gentleness, honoring healthy and appropriate timing. Always make sure you get the support you need. In other words, please focus solely on what you feel at peace with unearthing and exploring. That will be more than enough when it comes to practicing the tools and gaining greater confidence in your visibility.

Becoming Visible to Yourself by Using a Powerful Tool

Out beyond ideas of wrongdoing and rightdoing,
there is a field. I'll meet you there.—Rumi

To feel safe being seen by others, we must first be willing to truly see ourselves. This is what I call *becoming visible to yourself*—meeting your own gaze without the need to impress, without the armor of perfection, and without tucking away the parts you fear are too much or not enough.

At the end of each of the 28 lessons in this book, you'll find a gentle invitation: the video diary. These simple yet profound practices are a space for your truth to rise—unfiltered, unpolished, and unbridled. They offer a way to reclaim your voice, not by performing, but by witnessing yourself with honesty and compassion.

And the best part?

Video diaries are easy to do. All it takes is your presence, your voice, and a willingness to be seen—by you.

What is a video diary?

A video diary is like a journal—but instead of pen and paper, you offer your voice to the lens, not for the world, but for your own eyes and heart. It's a space to speak freely, to unravel your truth without the weight of being watched, judged, or polished. A sacred practice of becoming visible to yourself.

It's not about being impressive. It's about being real.

If the camera feels too vulnerable at first, try speaking in front of a mirror or into your phone's voice memo. The medium doesn't matter as much as your commitment to show up with honesty and curiosity. This is your space to speak without editing, without performance—a quiet excavation of your voice, layer by layer.

The diamonds will come—but first, we must sift gently through the rubble. This is where your truth lives.

Someone in my membership once shared, "I don't want to die without knowing myself." That stayed with me. Because truly, what if this isn't about anyone else at all? What if the real gift is simply this: *you, meeting yourself fully, unapologetically, in this lifetime*—and discovering the freedom and joy that come with expressing who you really are?

When we feel safe inside ourselves, that's when our voice becomes clear, magnetic, and deeply moving. Not because we're trying to be powerful—but because we are finally being real. It's in feeling deep safety inside ourselves as we show up authentically that we're able to confidently voice a message that moves others.

How do you create a video diary?

1. **Turn on your camera** (your phone is perfect).
2. **Look into the lens** as if you're speaking to your best friend—someone who makes you feel completely safe.

3. **Take a breath.** Feel your body. Listen within.
4. **Share without editing.** Even 30 seconds is enough—as long as you're present, tuned in, and real.
5. **End with a pause.** Place one hand on your heart, one on your belly, and breathe. Let your body feel safe through physical connection and your loving attention. This simple ritual creates a powerful link between expressing your truth and feeling grounded in yourself.

You'll receive a powerful nervous system tool on day 16. For now, let your video diaries be the gentle beginning—a way to whisper safety into your body each time you show up. With every word you speak, you're planting the roots of self-trust, so that whether you're alone in a quiet room or standing before a sea of faces, your body remembers:

I am home here.

It all begins with this simple, sacred start.

This practice may seem simple, and it is. When you commit to video diaries—on both good days and hard ones—it will steadily strengthen your self-trust, make speaking on camera feel like second nature, and grow your confidence from the inside out. At the end of each lesson, I give you a new video diary prompt to make communicating authentically on camera easier for you day by day and to help you see yourself through loving, present eyes.

I've had students who have had complete life and business transformations from this one tiny but mighty commitment for a full moon cycle. Twenty-eight days can be a portal from shrinking or holding back to confidently voicing your message that moves the world with video diaries alone.

Yvonne, a Decluttering Coach and student in my membership, is a perfect example of this. Here, she puts it in her own words:

"I had a lot of fear around expressing my truth freely, showing myself in group settings, and being seen as the beautiful, messy human that I am. As a recovering people-pleaser and perfectionist, I carried deep self-judgment and feared the judgment of others. My fear was, in essence, of losing love and belonging when I shine and show my whole self. My hope was to feel more free and confidently express the message within me. Recording video just for myself (video diaries) became a powerful tool for fostering intimacy and safety with myself. I let myself be seen—ugly in the morning, laughing, sad—without needing to edit or hide. That alone grew my self-confidence and sense of home within.

"I started falling in love with my own voice. That was very new as I used to not really like my voice on recordings. Over the past year I started to get compliments on the frequency of my voice. *Another big win is that I became visible with my soul business supporting women to free their home from clutter and freeing themselves through that.* I wrote my first newsletter and held my very first workshop. And made an offer at the end. It feels so good to be excited about what I'm doing and to have a clear purpose waking up each day."

As you can see, this practice can transform your confidence around sharing your voice. I want to make sure you jump on the video diary train because I've seen so many clients and students have their biggest breakthroughs by simply becoming visible to themselves. There is something that happens when you commit and make video diaries messily for your eyes only. They are guaranteed to help you in ways you can't imagine right now, especially while simultaneously using the tools I give you in this book.

LOVE NOTE: Please hold the 28 days of video diaries lightly and with patience. We're embarking on a transformative adventure. Think of this journey as being in the sandbox playing like you did as a small child. Give yourself permission to have fun, explore, and discover yourself. There's no way to do this wrong. You practicing being yourself and becoming visible to yourself is the big win, like finding treasure buried in the sand!

Phase I

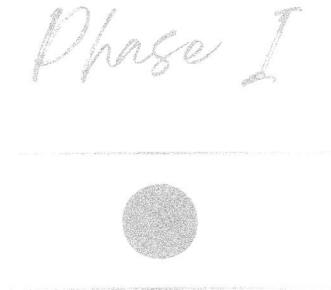

THE CALL TO BE SEEN

Day 1

The Call to Be Seen

*Everything changes when you start to emit your own
frequency rather than absorbing the frequencies around
you, when you start imprinting your intent on the
universe rather than receiving an imprint from existence.*
—Barbara Marciniak

This book is a divine appointment between you, me, and thousands of bighearted empaths, coaches, healers, and creatives who are reading alongside you. This is your clarion call to take up space, free your valuable voice, and more than anything, be the beacon of light you came here to be. Does that make your heart flutter?

Your knees tremble?

A smile emerge on your face?

Do you feel a sudden urgency to run for the hills?

Or curl up on your couch with a cup of tea as you devour these pages?

Whatever you feel, it's just energy—an aliveness returning. This is your time to overcome your greatest fears, choose yourself, and confidently shine.

There's ancient wisdom within you. Deep down you know it, but you may feel afraid. Later in this book, I'll reveal the bedrock of the fear that stops you so you can use it as a springboard into the self-love and self-confidence that powerfully sets your unique voice free.

One of my mentors, Steve Siler, says ...

I extend his wise words to you. *It's time to stop falling dark during dark times.* This is when you can shine the brightest. There are thousands of us throughout our beloved Planet Earth choosing presence, love, and compassion in good times and bad times like stars twinkling in a night sky.

This makes me think of Clare Telles, an intelligent, soul-centered woman in my membership who was widowed at a young age, raised her daughter as a single mom, buried the grief of losing her beloved husband by getting remarried, and ended up in a toxic second marriage that further destroyed her self-esteem and confidence. She was later diagnosed with stage 4 cancer, healed, and came out the other side a changed woman. She's a miracle! She learned to hear herself, understand her needs, and love herself deeply. She gained life-changing lessons and knew she had a lot of healing wisdom to share with others, but she was afraid of speaking in public due to growing up with a hypercritical mother who expected her to be perfect.

This is when she joined my membership to break through her visibility fears. I could see such potential in her, and in many ways she's my hero: living proof that people can come out of dire circumstances even more radiant, empowered, and loving than they were prior to facing them. Today, she has her own YouTube channel (@ClareTelles) and coaching business, where she uses her transformational story and transformational tools to help women thrive.

There are so many bighearted souls like Clare who, now more than ever, have the power to help humanity grow and evolve. There's a global hunger for what empaths naturally carry: compassion, wisdom, and authenticity. Nearly every empath I've ever met wants to help others and better our world. Empaths have some of the most giving hearts. There's a strong desire to leave this world a little brighter by the time we leave. To use what we've been through and our hard-won lessons to lessen the load on others who may be suffering through similar challenges. Does this sound familiar? Do you want to use what you've learned to help others?

Here's the thing: This call to serve also comes with something many empaths are shy or reluctant to admit: *a call to be seen.*

This call to be seen may seem like a practical one. Obviously, being seen is required in order to make what is being offered known to those you can offer it to. However, deep down, the call for empaths to be seen originates from a much deeper need than a utilitarian one.

This calling to help humanity evolve requires you to evolve first, and there's no faster way to evolve than by using the courageous path of visibility to clear fear, rewire your nervous system, and confidently voice your message that moves others.

To my surprise, guiding hundreds of empaths and sensitive leaders revealed that to be seen was really the soul's yearning to heal, release, and embody freedom.

Freedom from shrinking.

Freedom from silencing yourself to feel safe.

Freedom from feeling like a sponge that needs to hide to protect yourself from absorbing negative energy.

Freedom from the pain of quietly watching others do what you want to do from the sidelines.

Deep down, you yearn to be present and feel at home in your own skin no matter where you are or who you're with.

I call this your Evolutionary Why, which we'll get to. For now, I share this at the start of our journey to get to the heart of what your soul came to Earth for during these rapid evolutionary times—a deeper reason you may have picked up this book.

I believe empaths have this deep calling to be seen and share their voices because they are here to *heal, uplift, and awaken* others—but not just through their words or actions. Their very presence carries a compassionate energetic frequency that activates healing.

Why Empaths Feel Called to Visibility

1. **We are transmitters of healing energy.** Empaths often mistake themselves as sponges absorbing the energy of others. We didn't come here to be sponges. We're lighthouses! We're designed to be self-effulgent, shining from within. Empaths don't just share messages; we *embody* them and emit radiance. When we speak, write, or create, we transmit an energy that people *feel*—our visibility can be a form of energetic medicine.

2. **We are bridges between the seen and the unseen.** Many empaths are deeply intuitive, sensing things beyond the physical. Our insights help others navigate emotions, energy, and personal transformation. To fulfill this role, we are required to step forward and share what we know.

3. **Our stories create collective healing.** When an empath shares their truth, it often mirrors something in someone else, giving that person permission to heal, feel, and grow. Their courage to be seen *liberates others from their own fears*.

4. **We are here to shift the paradigm.** Many empaths feel as if we don't fit into traditional societal structures because we are here to *reshape* them. We don't fit into the current

limiting paradigm because we're here to create new ones, bringing in new ways of being, leading, and healing.

5. **Our souls remember something bigger.** This is the deep one. Many of us empaths feel a sense of destiny, as if our souls came here with a mission. Even if we don't have the exact words for it, we feel this inner pull to express, guide, and serve. Our visibility is part of our soul's evolution and contribution.

As empaths we look out at a troubled world and see the vast majority of people complacently adding to the problems with their bad news and addiction to fear, judgment, blame, and separation. We have solutions. We have good news. We have pathways to greater possibilities. We have messages that move the world. The call to be seen is not about *look at me, love me, validate me*. It's not about being in the spotlight; it's about *being* the spotlight, shining light on a message that serves people so that a healthier path is illuminated for others to walk if they choose. The only problem is that many empaths are riddled with fear, self-doubt, and overwhelm.

If you've ever dreamt of sharing your voice, but feel like you don't have anything valuable to share, imagine that your 15-year-old self just showed up. Pause. Take a breath. Imagine looking into their eyes. Would your heart have anything valuable to say to them? Dig deep into this. What would you guide her to do or not do? How would you speak with her? How would you listen? What would you applaud her for? What questions would you ask her? Can you see the value of the energy you bring to her? If not, don't worry. This book will help you more and more with each page so that you can truly own your worth.

Today's Video Diary Prompt

If your 15-year-old self were standing in front of you right now, what would you want her to know?

Day 2

The Reason Empaths
Play Small and Hide

Remember to show yourself compassion.
—Judith Orloff

ear of being visible and hiding out or playing small can usually be traced back to a time in your life when being fully alive and authentically expressed led to someone's upset, criticism, or discomfort. Our visibility fears today don't belong to our present selves, but rather to a younger child trembling inside our nervous systems who got frozen in history during a painful moment of perceived or blatant rejection. We almost certainly stopped breathing in such moments, unintentionally crystalizing a sense of danger any time the spotlight lands on us. Wanting to avoid visibility today is merely an echo of an earlier experience that shaped how we feel about being seen. It's understandable to want to push away potentially feeling rejected again.

Take a deep breath. I have good news for you.

Although it may sound hopeless, realizing visibility fears don't belong to your present self can actually be encouraging. Once you can see that you're innately self-assured and learn how to emerge as your most confident self, you'll be able to free yourself from visibility blocks.

There are seven core visibility blocks that are the result of foundational traumas, big and small, that arose when we spoke up or were the center of attention at an impressionable time of our lives. We'll be looking at all seven in the next section, where you'll also be uncovering which specific blocks you personally carry. Then in phase 3, you'll receive the solutions to set all seven blocks down.

In the previous chapter, we talked about the value and light you carry that can shine brightest during dark times. We explored the insights and gifts you came here to share with others. Yet, there are so many empaths who diminish themselves, disowning their worth, masking who they really are, and going invisible as a result.

Years ago, I worked with a powerhouse business coach—an assertive, successful leader who helped me quadruple my sales. She was a force, making many millions yearly, and I respected her. So, I started emulating her, believing that to reach her level, I had to look, sound, and lead like her. Over two years, my business soared, but a year later, I was hit with a health diagnosis that traced back to stress. That moment was my wake-up call. As I unraveled the truth, I realized my illness was rooted in a lack of self-worth—I had convinced myself that my softer, more empathic nature wasn't enough. I thought success required me to be bigger, bolder, louder. But in chasing someone else's version of success, I had lost my greatest wealth—my health!

Fortunately, I stepped off the speeding train, reclaimed my authenticity, and restored my health. Interestingly, by showing up without the hype or performance, my success continued to grow and, most importantly, I'm exponentially freer and more fulfilled than ever. Getting paid to be yourself—your real self—is a wonderful thing!

I share this story to help you see something important. If you feel like you're not good enough or you don't have the right look, the right age, the right credentials, the right voice, the right life story, the right eyebrows—by heavens, I've heard it all—to share your voice and help others, in some way you're robbing the very people who would benefit from learning from you. The mistake most people make is that they try to emulate a successful or popular person they admire. This leads to feeling small and afraid to be visible because it's exhausting to pretend and dismiss your unique worth.

Don't get me wrong. Sometimes it's valuable to model someone you admire if that helps you feel more confident at first and start your visibility journey. Don't be hard on yourself if you've done this, or are doing this. At some point, though, it's time to drop the pretense. You have your own unique energy, look, hard-won lessons, and way of expressing yourself that when set free will align you with your right community and your greatest success. Your people need you to be *you*. The Creator didn't make you one of a kind so that you'd try to be someone else. Imagine if you take all of that energy and put it into being the most real, empowered version of yourself. Look out, world!

You become unstoppable when you tell the truth about who you are—a child of the divine, a one-of-a-kind diamond!

Not believing in ourselves is a way of lying to ourselves, and the only place it gets us is … nowhere! Deep down you know that if you're to be seen sharing your authentic voice, you're going to be faced with the dragon of self-doubt, which is why there's such strong resistance, procrastination, and avoidance. I'm going to show you how to lasso the fear dragon and free your innate greatness so you can be energized by your visibility rather than depleted by the mere thought of it.

Empaths were never *meant* to shrink back or hide out. Our voices, energy, and presence are all part of the shift the world is craving. Rather than expecting the world to make you feel safe, a big part of this work revolves around what I call *becoming your own safety.* We'll go deep into this on day 15. For now, think about becoming your own safety as your #1 responsibility, particularly as you go for your dreams, sharing what you know, and living the life you came here to live. To lasso the fear dragon, I'll be inviting you to create a sense of safety for yourself as you do the thing you want to do, but are afraid to do. This is the formula for freedom!

The reason empaths play small and hide is because many are unknowingly lying to themselves about who they are, mistakenly basing their value on how well they fit into an abrasive society. To break through, you're being asked to discover and tell the truth about who you are—who you *really* are—rather than the version others expect you to be!

Your voice is valuable. Own it!

Your message is medicine. Sing it!

You've been playing small to feel safe, and that's okay.

Until it's no longer okay. You get incredibly offended when someone lies to you without owning the hard fact that you've been lying to yourself, pretending to be someone who isn't good enough. Maybe you've taken on a fearful character in a dark world who is powerless or victimized by it all. I know how deflating this is if you, someone who is here to bring the light during dark times, have fallen dark during dark times. It feels completely counter to who you truly are, because you're a messenger of something great, of something beautiful and holy. Your life story is full of value, lessons, and expertise. If you keep lying to yourself by continuing to tell the story of smallness, the only thing you protect is fear. If you keep hiding out, convincing yourself that this is what you want, when deep down you're yearning to expand, then fear is gripping the steering wheel of your life. Our job is to relax the grip, show some self-compassion, and step into a confident vibration so we can serve our pure, powerful messages, which I'm thrilled to help you do.

Today's Video Diary Prompt

When was the first time you remember feeling rejected while being 100% authentically yourself? What did you innocently make true about yourself, your visibility, or your life in that moment that has limited you?

Day 3

Vibrational Consequences of Hiding and Playing Small

*And the day came when the risk to remain tight in a bud
was more painful than the risk it took to blossom.*
—Anaïs Nin

ave you ever noticed that this calling to share your message and communicate something that inspires others won't let you go? Even if you've tried to hide out and silence your soul's voice, the desire keeps tugging at you like a wide-eyed child pulling at your sleeve, pointing toward a playground. "Look, look! Let's go!"

The reason the dream of sharing your message keeps returning to you is that it's meant for you. It's planted within you because you are the messenger. But, here's the thing. Your message is meant to be in the spotlight, not you. There is so much confusion in empaths given the nature of our *selfie* society. Fearing we're expected to step into the spotlight and present a certain image can make us cringe, wanting to hide and play small.

Let this be a relief.

Let this reorganize your energy so that you focus on something way beyond *me, me, me*.

Me is only the start of *message*!

What if your job is to simply be the messenger of the message, like someone delivering valuable cargo?

What if your real work is to shine a spotlight on your story that can move others?

Life has prepared you to inspire and empower others. Your life story, your insights, your energy, the way you look and speak—everything about you is what makes you the right messenger to reach the people who need the message from you. You don't need to perfect or change yourself. You're already the light. The spotlight on the song you're here to sing. No more preparation is needed at this point. Now it's simply about discovering how to feel safe being seen by clearing your visibility blocks (which we go deep into in phases 2 and 3 of this book). Your next step is learning how to feel comfortable in your own skin as you authentically share what can help others.

There is so much depression, anxiety, conflict, and malaise in the world. A huge reason for this collective turmoil is that people are plugged into *if it bleeds, it leads* fear-based news rather than their *lead with love* soul assignment. When we disconnect from what we love to do and get caught up in all the bad news, it's very easy to fall victim to the fear that we're being spoon-fed from nearly all directions. There's a chilling quote by Elizabeth Gilbert that says, "If I'm not actively creating something, then I'm probably actively destroying something." So many people feel like sh* (beep) because they're not creating. They're not sharing what's alive inside.

The first time I read Elizabeth Gilbert's quote, shivers shot up my spine. I realized the necessity of having a purposeful target, to be actively creating something that my heart wants. I read that quote when I was living alone in the redwood forest, moving through the dark night of the soul. I was being pummeled by self-destructive thoughts with no direction, feeling lost and afraid. I remember sitting at my meditation altar, my eyes swollen, face tight and salty from a layer of dried tears, and my nose raw from repetitively blowing it into a towel because it was the only thing thick enough to soak up the geyser of grief escaping my soul.

When I read that quote, I realized something important. The ego needs to be put to work so that it uses all of its mental power to build something meaningful rather than unnecessarily tearing things down, which was what was happening to me. I remember closing my eyes, feeling still after a big cry, and seeing a book in my mind's eye. I could feel the solidity of it in my hands. The four corners. The realness of it. I heard very clear guidance that I needed to write my story and describe the tools that were helping me heal. It didn't happen overnight, but I started jotting down ideas. Every time I thought about using what I had learned from facing emotional pain to build something purposeful that could help others, I felt more secure, and my vibration strengthened. I was starting to access the value I had to share. I was practicing overcoming the thoughts that belittled me and my vision of sharing my voice as an instrument for inspiration.

I remember someone close to me—wildly successful by the world's standards—once told me how noble he thought it was that I was willing to face my pain in order to heal. He was right. I *was* healing my life, something many people avoid like the plague. At the time, I was technically hiding out in the redwoods, tending to old wounds, but even then, a spark of light began to show me a larger vision: that one day, I would step into the spotlight and help others with the very truths I was uncovering in the dark. Being visible, serving your message, and living your deeper calling is a liberating way to create a thriving, confident life. This can feel foreign at first, given the world we live in where most people feel stuck in a dissatisfied life, secretly dreaming of something more, something truer.

You get to choose if you live your joy by living your mission. You get to choose if you show up as a light bringer during these dark times. You get to choose between clearing your visibility blocks so you feel calm in the spotlight or living with the gutting question: *What would have happened if I'd gone for it?*

I've had so many clients and students who hide or play small because they're afraid of being seen starting small or they don't want to risk being judged. They're trying to avoid being seen as a failure, an imposter, or imperfect. If you struggle with this, I'll give you the same good news I give them.

You cannot fail when you go for it! I know this firsthand. I pursued acting for nearly twenty years, and while the dream didn't give me the fulfillment I imagined, it gave me the courage, skills, and confidence I use every day in my work now. What looked like failure was actually preparation and redirection toward my true calling. When things don't work out the way you wanted, I guarantee you that you'll have gained necessary abilities and qualities to succeed at what your soul is navigating you to. The key is to go for what your heart genuinely desires now and trust you'll be led step by step to a level of fulfillment that is beyond your imagination. In later chapters, I'll help you with this.

For now, please take this in.

If things don't work out the way you envision them, you'll never have to bear the weight of the all-too-common question, *What would have happened if I would've had the courage to go for it?* Or the pang of regret. *What could have been?*

The guaranteed success you can grant yourself is that when you say *YES* to sharing your voice and fully bringing your gifts into the world, no matter what the outcome, you'll 100% grow and expand. You'll get to know yourself better and feel proud of yourself for living in courage and love rather than being tucked into cozy mediocrity driven by fear.

I once had a student who joined every one of my programs. She wanted to be visible. She wanted to find and express her voice. She dreamed of helping others using her unique stories, personal development tools, and teachings. But, she just couldn't get past her fear. She was self-conscious of her accent when she spoke English and judged herself as not having anything valuable enough to share. Sometimes she'd post something in our private membership and then she'd disappear for weeks. Then, during one of the modules in Confident Visibility School™, she had a sudden realization that cracked the shell around her, letting the light in and letting her light out.

She had an epiphany that one of the highest forms of self-love was to share her voice. She realized that sharing her authentic voice and getting to know herself in this way was such a joyful act for her that it was an act of self-love. Instead of trying to perform or get a result, she allowed her video diaries and visibility journey to be a way of caring for herself, hearing herself, and unearthing the gems she held inside like a child digging for treasure in the wild. From there, months later, as a natural byproduct she started making videos for others effortlessly. Everything she had been learning in Confident Visibility School™ and the membership clicked into place. She shot out like a cannonball, or better yet like a wild woman gleefully howling at the moon. It's a beautiful thing when an empath regains her confidence and claims her worth. She becomes a force—a loving force that moves the world into greater love!

You see, you never know when you're going to have your breakthrough. The key is to give yourself the dignity of being seen and heard imperfectly by becoming visible to yourself to start. This is why I encourage you to voice a video diary every day, as I emphasized in the introduction. The power of getting to know yourself in this intimate way, without pressure, perfectionism, or performance anxiety can unlock miracles for you.

In this beginning stage of our journey together, I want you to consider this:

What if you sharing your voice is for *you* and your freedom?

What if making an impact on others through sharing your voice is icing on the cake?

What if you and your own freedom are the cake itself!

Is that enough for you for now?

Today's Video Diary Prompt

Take a deep breath, place your hands on your heart, and imagine a loved one or pet you adore deeply. Let this energy build in your heart as you breathe. From this place, redirect this energy to yourself by asking your heart, *What do you want me to know today?* Then, open your eyes and spontaneously speak from love, looking straight into the camera and completing this prompt:

Sweetheart, what I want you to know today is …

Day 4

What Are Visibility Blocks?

Until you make the unconscious conscious,
it will direct your life
and you will call it fate.
—Carl Jung

ight now, as you hold this book in your hands, you also
hold a dream in your heart—a vision of helping others,
sharing your wisdom, and finally allowing yourself to be seen.
You imagine the deep fulfillment of voicing your hard-won
lessons and tools with the world, knowing they have the power
to change lives. You can feel the joy of waking up each morning
with purpose, doing work that lights you up, and being
abundantly supported in return. You see the faces of the people
you're meant to serve—grateful, inspired, transformed—
because of what you've shared with them.

You can picture yourself living with freedom, choosing where
and how you spend your days, designing a life that feels expansive
and aligned. No more fitting into someone else's expectations
or schedule. No more hiding parts of yourself to make others
comfortable. Just you—fully expressed, fully seen, fully thriving.

Or maybe, for now, the dream is simpler. Maybe you just want to feel at ease speaking up at a dinner party, confidently sharing your thoughts in a meeting, asking for a raise, or expressing yourself without second-guessing every word. Maybe all you truly long for is to set your authentic voice free—to feel the exhilaration of standing in your power, unapologetically, as yourself.

It feels good to imagine this being your life, doesn't it?

The real question is what's been stopping you.

You can come up with all kinds of reasons, or even examples from your life around why you've been holding back, hiding out, or postponing your dream. However, there's really just one reason at the bottom of it all: Visibility blocks have been stopping you.

What are visibility blocks?

Visibility blocks are internal barriers—often subconscious fears, beliefs, or emotional loops that prevent people from fully expressing themselves, being seen, and stepping into their soul-centered leadership. These blocks can manifest as fear of judgment, imposter syndrome, low sense of self-worth, perfectionism, or even a deep-seated belief that being visible is threatening and dangerous.

For an empath, coach, or creative, visibility blocks may specifically show up as:

- Fear of criticism or rejection—Worrying about what others will think if they share their truth.

- Self-doubt or imposter syndrome—Feeling like they're not *ready* or *qualified enough* to step into leadership.
- Energetic overwhelm—Feeling drained at the thought of being seen by many people at once.
- Fear of outshining others—Holding back because they don't want to make others uncomfortable.
- Past-life or ancestral wounds—A deep, intuitive fear that being seen is unsafe (perhaps because of persecution in past generations or overall in our human history).

No matter where we are on our leadership and life journeys, we all have visibility blocks running in our subconscious minds. They typically started at a very young age as the result of believing it's unsafe to be seen. These beliefs, having begun when we were quite vulnerable and impressionable, can silently run day after day, year after year, decade after decade, dictating our actions or pinning us into non-action as capable adults. This is why even when you consciously tell yourself you want to make videos and help others, or you want to take it to the next level, nothing changes unless visibility blocks are addressed.

Visibility blocks often begin forming between the ages of three and seven, when a child starts becoming aware of how they're perceived by others. This is the stage where they absorb societal, familial, and cultural conditioning about what is *acceptable* to express and what is not.

Many years ago in 2004, while getting a masters degree in spiritual psychology and studying psychological and developmental foundations, I was asked to explore my own childhood. During the coursework, I recalled a memory that I had completely forgotten about.

I was four years old and my mother had enthusiastically dragged me to an audition for a Disney World commercial. She put me in a colorful dress, patent leather shoes, and added a bow on top of my head. She blew out my hair, which was down to my waist. I looked like a doll—perfect for the part, but what she failed to understand was that I was a highly sensitive child. Walking into the thick-with-anxiety waiting room of the casting office, I could feel the avalanche of fears and pressures of the stage moms and their children there. I remember trying to stay composed in my pretty dress, but I could barely breathe. I kept a fixed smile on my face, pretending to be okay. Once they called my name and brought me into the auditioning room, I was expected to catch a big, bright beach ball, look to the camera and gleefully say, "I'm in Disney World!!" Well, as soon as they called *action*, my mother innocently peeked into the room to see how I was doing and I froze, locking eyes with her. The ball hit me in the head and the shame that came over me was paralyzing. This experience was the beginning of a visibility block that formed from the unconscious belief that I wasn't good enough, I couldn't do it, and therefore I was a failure.

Maybe you weren't four years old literally missing the ball in a Disney World commercial audition, but surely you've had a moment, or countless ones, when you innocently drew the conclusion that being center stage or fully expressed was a bad idea. Whether you carry a similar story of missing the mark and embarrassing yourself—like mine—or you have the opposite story where you nailed it and were given the star role in the school play, visibility blocks likely still formed, having parts of ourselves recoil and hide.

Let's say you got the solo and were center stage, giving the performance of the year in the elementary school play, and felt loved by your family, teachers, and peers because you did such a *perfect* job. This shaped you at a susceptible age. Everyone paid attention to you, which felt great, but unbeknownst to you, it started the block of perfectionism and believing that your value was based on being the best.

Like me, you may have had an experience where you felt like a failure or not good enough in a tender moment, and later in life learned to overcompensate by becoming a perfectionist.

Regardless of your unique story, we all have visibility blocks that were unconsciously formed at a time when we made innocent, limited assumptions about ourselves that just weren't true. The good news is that in becoming conscious of the origin of your visibility blocks, your mere awareness begins to diffuse their power, bringing more breath and life force into your body.

In the next chapter, we'll be exploring the seven core visibility blocks and starting to identify which have been weighing heavily on you, watering down your message, or silencing you altogether. In the third section, I'll be giving you easy, customized solutions for each block that work to clear them.

For now, let's set the stage by taking a breath, turning on your camera and completing today's video diary prompt for your eyes only. Remember, this is an opportunity to get to know yourself with neutral eyes and the curiosity of an explorer.

Let this be fun.

Let this be freeing.

Let this be your time to get to know yourself without judgment.

Today's Video Diary Prompt ✓

When was the *first time you remember feeling unsafe being fully expressed or the center of attention?*

Day 5

The Chakras and Seven Core Visibility Blocks

Each of the seven chakras are governed by spiritual laws,
principles of consciousness that we can use to cultivate
greater harmony, happiness, and well being
in our lives and in the world.
—Deepak Chopra

There are seven core visibility blocks. You may have one, several, or all. Whatever the case may be, becoming aware of your specific visibility fears will give you altitude so you can see and sidestep them, rather than being stuck in their grip. We'll be going deep into each visibility block and their solutions in upcoming chapters. For now, let's dive into a brief overview and explore exactly which visibility blocks currently have a hold on you.

Chakras are subtle energy storehouses located in the body that correlate with and affect different areas of our lives (for example, relationships, finances, self-esteem, self-expression, etc.). As you'll see in the following diagram, the first visibility block is located in the root chakra at the base of the spine, which influences your sense of safety, group connection, and belonging in the world. From there, the blocks move upward along the body's centerline, chakra by chakra, all the way to the crown of the head. You can use the diagram as a checklist to track the blocks you most identify with.

Illustrated by Glaiza Ganaba at Grid Creative Solutions

Seven Core Visibility Blocks

1. Vow of Smallness (root chakra)

This is the foundation of visibility blocks. "Small = safe" is the equation associated with this block. If this block could speak, it would confess (in a whisper, of course), "If I make myself tiny enough, then I'm safe because *if you can't see me, you can't hurt me*." This first visibility block is really a self-protective pattern—hiding, playing small, and guarding your truth out of fear of judgment or rejection. It's incredibly common, especially for empaths. Even those who seem confident may still be masking parts of themselves to feel accepted rather than showing up 100% authentic and bravely embodying their full radiance.

2. Busy Bee Block (sacral chakra)

The second core visibility block is the Busy Bee Block. You know you have this block if you're always too busy, overwhelmed, or stretched to make space for what your soul really wants to explore and share with others.

If you're always busy, doing for others, and rarely have time for yourself, this is a key block to look at. Feeling tired but wired, ungrounded, or rushing from one thing to the next—what I call *nexting*—can quietly sabotage your confidence and creative visibility. For empaths who struggle to slow down, receive, or just *be*, this Busy Bee Block often masks deeper feelings or unmet needs hiding beneath the motion.

3. *Not Enough* Trance (solar plexus chakra)

The third core visibility block is the *Not Enough* Trance. It's an unconscious program that says, "I'm not valuable enough. I'm not good enough. No matter what I do, I'll never be enough!"

This is indeed a trance—a trance of negativity that's hypnotizing our culture. Have you ever felt like you were lacking something, or judged yourself as a downright failure? You have this great inspiration to do something, and then suddenly doubt kicks in and says, *Who am I to do this?* The Not Enough Trance is a wound of identity. If you hold back because you feel too much or not enough, you've likely lost touch with your true self. This pattern often begins in childhood, when being fully yourself didn't feel safe or was met with judgment. So, you learned to hide, shrink, or shape-shift—forgetting your innate worth in the process.

4. Bleeding Heart Block (heart chakra)

The fourth core visibility block is the Bleeding Heart Block. The Bleeding Heart Block is a codependent terror of unintentionally hurting others, someone taking your message the wrong way, or getting pushback when sharing your authentic voice.

Think of this block as a cage: the people-pleaser, good-girl cage. It keeps you silent by having you believe *I can only be good, and I have to please others. Anything outside of that is forbidden, a threat, or dangerous.* If you were the peacekeeper or experienced bullying growing up, you may carry a deep fear of upsetting others. For empaths, this can feel like a cage—where shining fully feels unsafe unless everyone else is okay. This block stems from over-responsibility and a quiet belief that your truth must stay hidden to keep the peace.

5. Persecution Wound (throat chakra)

The fifth core visibility block is the Persecution Wound, or the Witch Wound. This is a collective spiritual trauma carried through generation after generation when people were killed for having healing gifts. Women were killed for sitting in the forest alone meditating. Wisdom keepers were hung for sharing deeper truths and spiritual energy. Thousands of people were annihilated for expressing insights that came from tapping into the intuitive, feminine realms.

If your throat tightens when you try to speak, or you feel deep resistance to being visible—especially with your spiritual or intuitive voice—you may be carrying the Persecution Wound. This wound often shows up as fear of being seen, losing your train of thought, or not knowing where to begin because your wisdom feels too vast. You might feel blocked, like your voice is stuck in your throat, even though you're connected to something sacred and powerful. For many empaths, this isn't just personal—it's a collective trauma of being silenced, misunderstood, or punished for speaking from the soul.

6. Comparison Cage (third-eye chakra)

The sixth core visibility block is the Comparison Cage. Have you ever compared yourself to others, diminishing yourself in some way or maybe even judging them?

You know you're stuck in the Comparison Cage if you're watching what everyone else is doing from the sidelines, and you're thinking to yourself, *Oh my God, they're sharing the exact same thing I'd be sharing, and they're doing it more powerfully, have a huge audience, and they even look better doing it.* If you're stuck in this visibility block, it can create so much tension in your head and neck because rather than freely expressing yourself, your mind is churning in patterns of overthinking.

The Comparison Cage either has you feeling inferior to others, putting them on a pedestal, or smugly criticizing them, thinking you can do a better job, while watching silently and staying invisible.

You know the Comparison Cage has you cornered if you face any of these scenarios:

- You feel inferior as you compare yourself to others, and it painfully keeps you hiding
- You feel superior to others who are visible, judging them, but are not visible yourself
- You struggle with jealousy as you watch others sharing while painfully staying on the sidelines

7. Perfectionist Headlock (crown chakra)

The seventh core visibility block is the Perfectionist Headlock, and yes, it's a headlock. When the perfectionist is running the show, it's like being caught in the armpit of a world-champion wrestler. You know you're caught in the headlock if you keep dreaming of sharing your voice, but you just can't do it. Even though you know you want to go for it, you keep procrastinating.

If you have this kind of narrative in your head that says, *I can't share until it's perfect!*

Until …
my branding is perfect
I look perfect
my message is perfect
my website is perfect
my body is perfect
I have the perfect credentials and get another certification …
blah, blah, blaaaaaah deeeeeeblah … then this one has got you. Unless the Perfectionist Headlock is released, that stinky pit will hold you back forever, because perfect doesn't exist.

Now that you have an overall idea of all seven visibility blocks, it's time to have fun answering today's video diary prompt below. In letting yourself speak freely without the edit button, you just might unearth valuable insights about yourself you didn't expect.

Today's Video Diary Prompt

Out of the seven core visibility blocks, which ones have been stopping you and which one do you feel has been limiting you the most?

Day 6

Where Do Visibility Blocks Come From and Where Do They Live Now?

The cave you fear to enter holds the treasure you seek.
—Joseph Campbell

In recent years, science has proven that we store past experiences, including emotional energy and memories, in our bodies. Healers, sages, and shamans have known this for ages, but there's finally measurable evidence that confirms the mind-body connection.

Why does this matter to you and your journey into confident visibility? Because …

The body holds information that shapes how safe or unsafe being seen feels. This is why many people can suddenly feel anxiety in their physical bodies without having fearful thoughts or undergoing problematic situations.

For years, I'd get on stage as an actress and black out, not remembering what happened. My body would go through the motions, but I was not in my body, so I had zero recollection of what happened while all eyes were on me. It took me opening up to deep healing work to realize that the fear and shame I felt at four years old when the ball hit my head during the commercial audition were lodged in my nervous system, along with other memories and feelings.

To put it plainly, the emotional charge behind visibility blocks comes from the past (usually childhood) and currently resides in your body. It's why you may find yourself feeling unsafe in your own skin when speaking in front of others, while around certain people, or in a specific environment.

I have sat with client after client in Confident Course Creation VIP days, and as soon as I set up the camera to film them, they often go from shining to shrinking. They'll even say things like, "I know it's in my head, and I just need to get over it!"

But here's the truth ...

This is why we've gotten so good at escaping into our heads through overthinking. What's going on in your head is an escape route from what's repressed in your body. Often, your body is being reminded of a past perceived threat (even if your mind doesn't consciously remember) and it's sending a danger signal to hold off or stop altogether in a perfectly safe situation. Feeling like you're in danger, whether it's life-threatening or ego-threatening, is what leads to fight-or-flight syndrome (aka avoidance of feeling through thinking), and discomfort in the body.

It's a domino effect:

1) Danger signal, 2) Avoid feeling through overthinking, 3) Emotion hardens in the body.

These hardened blockages in our physical and emotional bodies are what I call RUBBLE, an acronym for repressed unconscious beliefs and blocks of locked emotion. I go deep into this in my first book, *The Diamond Process™: Using Everyday Triggers to Awaken the Treasure Within*. The more *rubble* we carry, the more we try to escape the body and find ourselves imprisoned in thinking—serving time in the mind, so to speak. It's very difficult to exit this prison without using tools that work. This is why most people, rather than serving their love-filled messages, become slaves to fearful narratives that keep them hiding out.

The toolkit I give you in this book will help you consciously chisel away the rubble rather than fearfully lock it in. These same tools have helped hundreds of my students and clients to reveal the masterpiece within and sculpt the message they came here to share! I'm thrilled to hand these to you, too! I want to be clear about something, though. This 28-day journey we're on together is not about adding anything to yourself. It's about emerging from the rubble. Deep down you know you already have everything you need within yourself to confidently shine. This journey is about unburdening yourself from the blocks and freeing the value that's already within you, like excavating a diamond from the rough.

I want to share a metaphor with you. It perfectly illustrates that what you want is already within you and the work is to chisel away what is not you.

In 1501, in the heart of Florence, Italy, one of the greatest artists of all time, Michelangelo, was commissioned to carve a massive, narrow block of Carrara marble that had been abandoned for over 40 years in a courtyard, dismissed as unusable. Two artists had already attempted to shape it into the figure of David, only to abandon their efforts, deeming the stone too flawed, too difficult to work with. For years, it remained untouched—until Michelangelo saw what others could not. He accepted the challenge and brought the neglected slab into his studio. With each strike of his chisel, he carved away everything that was not David, revealing the masterpiece hidden within. When asked how he had created such perfection from an imperfect stone, he simply replied, "I saw the angel in the marble and carved until I set him free."

Michelangelo didn't impose his vision upon the marble—he uncovered what was already there. His masterpiece was never about force, but about liberation. He completed the sculpture in 1504, transforming something *worthless* into one of the greatest masterpieces in history.

This story isn't just about sculptures and art, it's about you and your message. How many years have you let yourself and your sacred calling remain hidden, falsely labeled as not good enough? Has it been 20, 30, 40 … 70 years? The real question is whether you want to stay labeled and stuck in a mental junkyard or be liberated into loving your life and sharing your valuable voice.

Since you picked up this book, you've already chosen the latter. Now, how do we effectively free ourselves like Michelangelo freed the angel in the marble?

Sending your body safety signals is what helps the nervous system soften and relax when it misinterprets a healthy situation as a dangerous one. For example, if you're eager to make a video, but your palms sweat or your voice quivers so you can't get the words out, there is a way through.

And guess what?

It's NOT by pushing harder, heavens no!

We've been programmed to *man up!*, muscle through, crush it … or just give up altogether, but that never resolves the root issue—limiting beliefs and energetic blockages lodged in the body.

When you realize that anything resembling a past negative imprint (or anything outside your comfort zone, for that matter) could trigger unprocessed emotions from the past, preventing you from going for your dreams, the path becomes clear and relief sets in.

Committing to a new way of relating to your body's sensations, listening and responding to her language, and effectively releasing repressed emotions become the essential way forward … just as essential as Michelangelo's chisel.

This new relationship with your body sets a foundation to clear the fear from your body so it becomes easy for you to confidently share your beautiful message once and for all.

The real work is in migrating out of self-defense, overcoming hypervigilance when fear gets triggered, and mindfully grounding into your body instead. A big part of this is treating your body like a temple. You are being asked to receive the good in your life—healthy food, sunshine, fresh air, movement, loving community, support, wisdom teachings, play, beauty rituals that help you feel radiant, and space to hear your soul—so you can be the frequency of the good news. Having a compassionate, present relationship with your body, including your emotional body, is not only the doorway into confidence when you take center stage to be a messenger of your message, it's how to fall in love with life. This journey into confident visibility is an invitation to expand your capacity to receive, master the art of harmonizing your nervous system, and set your potential free.

One thing to consider: When someone has spent their whole life overthinking, worrying, and fearing their feelings, being present doesn't feel safe to a body that's been programmed to run fast from pain. So, I'm asking you to please make space, be extra gentle with yourself, and be patient with this process.

You're in bloom, and blossoming cannot be forced!

Today's Video Diary Prompt ☑

If visibility blocks live in my body, the first place I sense these fears exist in my body is _____, and if they could speak, they would say ....

An Unconventional Way to Instant Confidence: Your Evolutionary Why!

Yesterday I was clever, so I wanted to change the world.
Today I am wise, so I am changing myself.
—Rumi

There have been so many moments on my visibility journey when I've wanted to quit.

I've stared at my YouTube dashboard, questioning everything. I've looked at videos that barely moved the needle—no flood of comments, no rise in subscribers, no financial return—and thought, *What's the point?* I'd pour my heart into a message that felt sacred, only to be met with silence. And in those moments, a familiar inner voice would whisper, *You're not growing. No one's listening. This isn't working.*

It happened over and over. A video would land with a thud, and I'd spiral into self-doubt. I was measuring my worth by external metrics: likes, comments, views, money, growth. And when those numbers didn't reflect the soul I was putting into my work, I felt invisible.

But what I didn't expect was that the opposite could feel just as toxic. Some videos brought in waves of engagement—tons of comments, shares, subscribers, excitement. One video unexpectedly attracted years worth of my most ideal students and filled a six-figure program. But those highs were just as destabilizing, because I found myself chasing that feeling, trying to replicate the result, and needing the next video to hit just as hard. I was bewitched by external wins. My nervous system would spike with pressure to *keep it up*, and suddenly, I wasn't creating from freedom—I was performing from fear of losing what I'd gained.

But here's the thing: Most creators will tell you the same truth—some videos pop, while most have average results. The rhythm of creating is not always loud or visible. It's often quiet. But I wasn't seeing that. I was holding myself hostage to the outer response, and in doing so, I kept abandoning the part of me that just wanted to *sing*—like a bird sings, not for applause, not for validation, but because the song is alive inside and must be sung.

It wasn't until I began to shift the *reason* I was making videos that everything began to change.

I stopped doing it to get something.

I stopped doing it to prove something.

I even stopped doing it to help or transform the world.

I started doing it to *free myself.*

To speak my truth because it mattered to *me*.

To make visibility an empowering practice, not a performance.

And that's when I discovered the easiest way to confident visibility, what I now call your Evolutionary Why.

What is an Evolutionary Why?

Your Evolutionary Why is the deeper soul-driven reason for sharing your voice. It's not rooted in metrics, applause, or even impact—it's rooted in growth, healing, and freedom. It's the why that says, *I show up not to succeed, but to evolve. I use visibility as a tool to become more of who I truly am as I commit to voicing something of value that could potentially help someone.*

As an empath, healer, or heart-led coach, this shift changes everything. When your nervous system gets activated around being seen, it's not a sign you're failing—it's an invitation to become your own safety. Your visibility becomes a spiritual practice: an edge where your fear meets your healing. We'll be going deep into this on day 15.

Here's the magic I want you to hold today:

You can't fail at this kind of visibility I'm suggesting to you.

Even if no one watches.

Even if your voice trembles.

Even if you mess up your words.

If you show up with *self-compassion*—if you're kind to yourself in the process—then confidence builds naturally. Your nervous system recalibrates. Your soul expands. You grow stronger every time you show up, not in perfection, but in truth.

Your Evolutionary Why becomes your gateway to true confidence because it's no longer about what impresses others, but about liberating you.

The Real Win That Gives You Instant Confidence

When your win becomes your own *courage*, your own *consistency*, your own *truth expressed*—then visibility becomes a playground of liberation, not a performance stage of pressure. And ironically, that's when people feel you and are most drawn to you. That's when your presence starts to land for them. That's when they can hear and receive your wisdom. Not because you're trying to be something, but because you've stopped. You've quit playing a part—a part that pulled you apart from your whole self—and instead you speak calmly from your heart.

And the thing is, when you *don't* show up, when you stay hidden out of fear of failing, you miss one of the greatest opportunities available to you—the chance to grow rapidly through the act of being seen and committing to healing your visibility wounds along the way.

It's natural to feel exposed and emotionally stirred when being visible, especially at first. Almost every time I film a video, I have the urge to take it down. The fear-based thoughts rush in: *That wasn't good. It wasn't valuable. I should just delete it.* But I've made a deal with myself that I don't take my videos down—because some are average, some are great, and the truth is, *I'm* all of it. I'm average sometimes. I'm great sometimes. I share this because so many people keep their gifts locked away because of the fear that what they create isn't enough or will be judged. There's gold in all of us. And it brings this sinking feeling to my heart to think of that brilliance being hidden behind limiting assumptions and beliefs about what success is.

Even the most impressive artists fear the spotlight on them— Meryl Streep has been known to pace and perspire. She openly admits being overwhelmed by the pressure of public appearances. These fears of inadequacy are normal as a way of avoiding public humiliation. What matters is not letting them stop you. I've learned that when I'm not focused on what I can get—more likes, more approval, more subscribers—I'm free to create and give from love. That's when I can show up for the one person who might hear my message and say, "I needed that." And that's worth everything. I often make the distinction between a follower of fear and a Leader of Love. A follower of fear is focused on being flawless. It's all about *me, me, me* and trying to be seen in a certain light! Being a Leader of Love means being willing to show up in your mess and your magic, your brilliance and your average. It's all about what you can give, not get—this includes giving acceptance and safety to yourself as you share. And in this beautiful and intentional way, you can use visibility as a rapid path of personal growth, freedom, and evolution.

Today's Video Diary Prompt

Now that you've had a week of video diaries, let's take inventory.

What repeat patterns, discoveries, or learnings have come up for you in the video diaries you've done so far?

Love note: If you've read the video diary prompts but haven't started them yet, it's okay. This is why we're regrouping on video diaries now. This is your moment to commit so you can receive the benefits from this powerful practice. Start with one video diary. Even if it means looking into the lens and saying, "I have no idea how to do this or what to say," notice where being honest takes you.

Phase II

UNCOVERING YOUR
VISIBILITY BLOCKS

Day 8

Vow of Smallness

Step out of the shadows. Let your presence be felt.
—Oprah

*N*ow we begin the sacred work of uncovering your specific visibility blocks—those quiet, hidden patterns that have kept you from fully stepping into your light. Over the next seven chapters, I'll guide you through one block each day. With gentle curiosity, you'll explore which ones live within you, not to judge or fix, but to understand. Awareness is the first doorway to transformation.

Then, in the next section of the book, we'll dive into the remedies—what I call the Seven Facets of Confident Visibility—each one designed to help you reclaim your voice, your presence, and your power.

The Vow of Smallness

Today, we start at the root.

The first and most foundational visibility block lives in the root chakra, at the base of the spine. This energy center is governed by our most primal need: to belong. To feel safe. To know we won't be cast out for being who we are.

This is where we meet what I call the Vow of Smallness—the deeply ingrained belief that it's safer to shrink than to shine. That staying quiet means staying protected. That dimming our light will help us avoid judgment or rejection. While this unconscious vow may have once helped us survive, it no longer serves the version of you who's ready to thrive.

Fear of being judged and rejected is the engine that keeps this vow roaring, coughing up smoke, and keeping many talented empaths choked into silence.

Surprisingly, in many surveys, including the Chapman University Survey of American Fears, the number one fear reported isn't death—it's public speaking. That's right: More people are afraid of being seen and heard than of dying. Comedian Jerry Seinfeld once joked that at a funeral, most people would rather be in the casket than giving the eulogy. For empaths, this fear often runs even deeper, as visibility can feel like emotional exposure and lead to a vulnerability hangover. But beneath the fear of public speaking often lies a more primal fear—the fear of rejection, of not belonging, or of *dying* symbolically in the eyes of others. Understanding this can help us meet our visibility fears with compassion rather than shame.

Psychologists say public speaking isn't just about words; it's about visibility, vulnerability, and the risk of being cast out. Rejection feels like a kind of social death. Failure is an ego death. Isolation? It's the ache of fading out or being irrelevant, a symbolic death. But when we recognize these as echoes of a deeper longing—to matter, to be safe, to be loved—we can understand our needs better and begin to step forward with self-compassion. This is what the next section of this book will help you with. First, let's go deeper into exploring this foundational visibility block. Awareness, in and of itself, will gradually start to dissolve it.

The Vow of Smallness is defined by an energetic equation I refer to as *small = safe.* What that means is I unconsciously take a vow or make a commitment at some point in my life, usually childhood, that I am going to stay very small, because if I am small, I will be safe. It's an unconscious agreement that sees hiding out as the safest bet. Its mantra is: *If you can't see me, you can't hurt me.*

If you have this block running, you likely silence your voice or hide out in some shape or fashion. It may not be everywhere and with everyone, but it may be in one particular place in your life with a certain group of people. I can assure you that if you have this block, even if solely with one particular person whose opinion holds weight for you, the very last thing you'll do is choose to be on video or in the public eye, or you'll run yourself into the ground as you go for it. You may secretly want to share your authentic voice in some way or grow a dream business, but the fear of rejection overrides it.

The problem with this is if we have this avoidance pattern running and we simultaneously have a competing intention to share our work with the world, then the Vow of Smallness is going to destroy our plans. It's like having one foot on the gas and one on the brake—not a good outcome for the car! A lot of autoimmune diseases stem from this self vs. self inner battle.

I know firsthand because it took me facing my own version of this to see how my unconscious adherence to the Vow of Smallness was hurting me. Ironically, I was very visible with 20,000+ YouTube subscribers and a six-figure business doing what I love. The Vow of Smallness can affect you at any stage. Although I was confidently sharing my message and doing high-value work with clients and students, behind the scenes I was running myself into the ground in fear-based control patterns. Unbeknownst to me, I didn't feel safe being successful. Unconsciously, I felt like a bad person for making great money doing meaningful work, and having complete time and location freedom while most people were struggling and stressing. It felt threatening to be seen as a leader living such a charmed life by so many people, as if I could become a target. Instead of addressing or even noticing my anxiety, I pushed harder so I could prove how hard I was working like everyone else. So I could fit in. The pattern was so subconscious that I didn't know it was running.

Grind culture is so prevalent in our society that I interpreted my anxiety as the excitement of being driven. This *kill it-crush it-be the best* mentality was praised and modeled by those I respected, including my own business coach. So, I ignored the feelings of danger in my nervous system and used action to sweep the discomfort away. Thank goddess, a health diagnosis cornered me out of nowhere following decades of textbook perfect health. And yes, I sing loud and proud—*thank goddess for that health diagnosis!!* You read that right. The frightening numbers in my bloodwork were the wake-up call I needed to choose myself and change the way I do my life, my visibility, and my business. I ended up reducing my work to 25% of what I had been doing previously and putting most of my energy into my own healing, part of which involved becoming my own safety (which is the solution to this block—more on that soon). For now, just keep in mind that without clearing this visibility block, no matter how hard we try, it's going to be nearly impossible to feel genuine calm and confidence in the spotlight so we can flourish going forward.

Overthinking Leads to Shrinking

One of the ways we stay small is through overthinking. Overthinking is a sure way to shrink your energy and dim your light. It's a tactic the ego uses to avoid uncomfortable feelings like terror, grief, and rage. I remember waking up in the middle of the night in a panic for two months straight the year before my health diagnosis. My mind would spin in fearful thoughts, ruminating over worst-case scenarios during a huge growth spurt in my business. As a deep sleeper, I knew something was systemically wrong. I was feeling out of control because my financial and class-size numbers were getting bigger and bigger. I felt like my business and my livelihood were in danger because I no longer had the bandwidth to spoon-feed every student who came into my programs.

I felt like I was going to be attacked, and as fate would have it, I ignored the warning signals when a psychologically troubled student enrolled in a program. Rather than confronting, refunding, and removing her from the program, I played small and avoided the situation because I was afraid of rocking the boat. Having grown up with an emotionally unstable mother, my people-pleaser patterns got the best of me to keep the peace. Months of going against my knowing cost me my health in the end. Yet, it gave me a million-dollar lesson in the process of reclaiming my health: Revoke all vows of smallness and do the work required to feel safe in my own skin as I stand in my power and live in integrity no matter how anyone sees me.

If you have this foundational block running, which is ultimately a fear of rejection, imagine how unstable it would feel to be visible or grow beyond a certain point of outward success.

No matter how much accountability you have or how much you learn, it's going to be very hard to put yourself out there if you unconsciously believe your safety depends on the approval of others. It's a tribal fear that says, *If you accept me, I'm safe. If other people accept me, then I belong to the tribe and will survive.* The problem with this is that when fitting in requires hiding facets of yourself, you might survive, but you can't thrive. As my wise acupuncturist Dr. Yvonne Farrell says, "It's not possible to flourish when you're habituated to self-defense."

In essence, this first visibility block is a commitment to hiding out, guarding yourself, and playing small due to a fear of being judged, harmed, or rejected. This can be unbearably painful, especially when you have lived through big lessons that can be of great value to others.

The Vow of Smallness is the most common block that affects nearly everyone. Even seemingly confident people can carry this one in a camouflaged form, presenting as self-assured but hiding genuine facets of themselves to gain popularity.

If you believe that you can't be okay unless others accept you, you'll have to shrink, fragment, or falsify yourself in order to fit in. If this is you, don't worry. There's a way through. I'll be sharing the solution with you in phase 3, after we explore all seven core visibility blocks.

Today's Video Diary Prompt ☑

If you allow yourself to be seen, what are you most afraid of happening?

Busy Bee Block

Many of us spend our whole lives running from feeling with the mistaken belief that you can not bear the pain. But you have already borne the pain. What you have not done is feel all you are beyond that pain.
—Kahlil Gibran

One of the most common visibility blocks is something I call the Busy Bee Block, which energetically lives in the second chakra, in the pelvic region between the navel and the pubic bone. This chakra is ruled by sexuality, passion, and creativity. You know the Busy Bee Block is limiting you if you're overwhelmed and don't have time for yourself and what you dream of creating.

Have you ever felt wired, buzzing about with anxious energy, going from one thing to the next—but deep down you're exhausted and maybe even sad, yearning for space? This is called being tired and wired. It's very common amongst ambitious types and driven empath entrepreneurs, for example. Feeling like you're always behind and there's never enough time is hard on the body, especially the nervous system. The Busy

Bee Block may look productive on the surface, when usually it's neurotic energy driving one's life. When unchecked, this block can become harmful to the physical body because there's never enough calm and stillness to replenish.

The real struggle that's driving the Busy Bee Block is a fear of feeling uncomfortable emotions. It's an intimacy issue that leads to getting too busy to have any time to face difficult feelings with another or with ourselves. When met with a troubling person or event, have you ever found yourself saying, "I don't have time for this!"? This is the Busy Bee Block's mantra, and its directive is to stay in constant action and overdrive to avoid vulnerability.

Whenever I help clients create their Soul Signature Course, their unique body of work, in Confident Course Creation School™, they often go full throttle with the creation process. Their energy can feel like a wild horse shooting out from the gate after being locked up for ages. I remember being in a private session with a client who was giving me an update on everything she had done that month.

"I finished all the modules—check!

"I filled out all the Create Sheets—check!

"I wrote my entire course—check!

"I printed it out—check!" as she waves a thick stack of pages in a folder.

"I did the …"

"Wait!" I stop her in her tracks. "Before you move on, am I hearing you correctly? Is that your Soul Signature Course in those pages?"

"Yes."

"Can you please pick them up and take a moment to really breathe in what you've created here?"

Her eyes widen. It had never occurred to her to pause and take inventory of her feelings.

I continue. "Your wisdom … this body of work has been sitting in your soul for decades, and now you have a valuable system you can help clients with. How does it feel?"

Next thing you know, her unblinking eyes burst into tears. The happiest tears you've ever seen. She's never paused long enough to own what's she's created, how she's living her truth and her deeper purpose after years of living out other people's expectations of her. She hadn't celebrated herself until I had her set down her to-do list for a moment and take in the present moment. When she slowed down, the feelings raced through her, welling up as tears in her eyes within seconds, like a chained thoroughbred horse suddenly set free. Sometimes, the Busy Bee Block is not only in place to keep us from feeling pain, but also from feeling too much joy.

One of the most common ways I see this block show up is when clients and students turn on their cameras to film their course lessons, sales page videos, or marketing content. They often fall silent, terrified of being judged, and like clockwork get too busy to do this part of the work. They avoid being visible, promoting their new course, and enrolling students. It's a perfect way for the subconscious to sweep away and bury big emotions, because if people can't see you, they can't judge you.

Most people unconsciously hide and hush themselves because they don't know what to do with the discomfort, anxiety, and shame that often comes with being seen and heard.

Don't worry, we'll be getting to a clear and simple solution. For now, I encourage you to check in and see if you're perpetually running out of time, feeling behind, or doing things for everyone else but never have enough time for yourself and what you want to create. If so, this is a primary block for you to clear. If you feel ungrounded and a bit spun out, racing to the next thing and the next thing, spiraling in what I called *nexting*, then this block is sabotaging your confidence, visibility, and potential. It may also be sabotaging your income because, let's face it, if people can't see you, they can't buy from you. If you're busy with big projects that you need to get done, keeping your dream work or deeper art submerged, this block may be furtively overruling your creative life.

To summarize in simple terms, the real issue here is one of intimacy. The Busy Bee Block may be pointing to you not being grounded in your body because you're unwilling to feel your feelings. If you have this one, then you might even fear voicing your genuine needs. Your comfort zone is possibly being needed by others, even though you might resent it at times.

If you're a hard worker, overachiever, or find it difficult to just be, receive, and enjoy the moment, then welcome to the world of the Busy Bee Block. Moving through life without any space to pause is often an unconscious escape to avoid deeper feelings and unmet needs.

Your feelings and unconscious beliefs may get amplified when sitting in front of a camera, or stepping into the spotlight. Being visible is going to pull up all of those fears—what I call RUBBLE (repressed unconscious beliefs and blocks of locked emotion). I know it may sound dreadful, but guess what?! This is great news when you know how to move through the fears and release the *rubble*, because it leads to freedom and deep confidence … which is where we're headed.

Today's Video Diary Prompt ☑

The feeling I don't want to feel and resist at all costs is the feeling of _____ because _____.

Day 10

The *Not Enough* Trance

It's not your job to like me, it's mine.
—Byron Katie

There is a core visibility block that affects the majority of people, and it's founded on the belief of not being good or valuable enough. I call it the *Not Enough* Trance because it acts like a trance, hypnotizing a person into feelings of worthlessness and even self-loathing. When this trance of negativity overtakes the mind, it muffles the brilliance that's innately within talented coaches, artists, healers, and all kinds of empaths who are here to bring something beautiful, inspiring, and valuable to others.

This visibility block is associated with the third chakra, which is our energy center of personal power. It has a lot to do with our self-esteem and how we see or relate to ourselves. If you have this area of your life blocked, self-doubt is likely a noisy companion rattling around in your mind.

If the Not Enough Trance has got you in its spell, you may have thoughts like:

- Who am I to make videos or speak about this subject?
- I'm nothing special.
- I don't have enough credentials or expertise.
- I'm too big/too small.
- My story is too dramatic to share.
- I hate my voice. I sound like a child/I sound too commanding.
- No one is going to care. I don't even have an audience.
- I'm too old/too young.
- I'm not pretty enough/too pretty to be taken seriously.
- I'm going to make a fool of myself.

All of these are exactly the same block: believing you're not enough or too much, which are two sides of the same coin. Can you see how there's no way to win when you're under this painful spell?

The Not Enough Trance burdens you with a skewed way of seeing yourself. When you've got the volume turned up on its critical narrative, it keeps you from realizing how powerful you are. If you don't have a sense of your worth and feel like a fraud or an imposter, you will continue hiding out and avoiding sharing your valuable voice. Essentially, you end up robbing your audience from the healing, insights, and inspiration they would gain if you believed in yourself enough to generously share what you've learned.

If this is running for you, or if you feel a low sense of self-esteem or lack of self-worth, then there's a distortion or imprint that interrupted your confidence in your authentic self, often during childhood. Somewhere along the way, being in your full glory or just being naturally you got you in trouble. So, you chose to hide, dim, shrink, and forget who you really are by trying to turn yourself into something else or disappear completely.

I personally picked this one up during my epic fail at four years old during the Disney World commercial audition, which took me 30+ years to get conscious and clear of. If you don't realize how powerful you are, believe that life is happening *to* you instead of *for* you, or you think the authority of your life is outside of you, then you likely have this trance as your default mindset. A great example of this is waiting or hoping for someone to discover or rescue you. These are prime examples of displaced power. Do you secretly wish someone in a position of power or authority would validate you so you can finally go for it and forge forward? If so, let's throw the confetti, high five, and uncork a great bottle of kombucha or Brut Nature champagne. You're making the unconscious conscious, which is where deep confidence begins!

I remember when I moved to Los Angeles in 1998 as a bright-eyed 21-year-old with big hair and a big dream of being a big-shot actress. I'd strut—and I do mean full-on catwalk strut—into parties, night clubs, and industry events secretly hoping to be discovered. At that time, the power always felt like it was outside of me in casting directors, movie directors, acting teachers, famous actors, or anyone with influence in the film business. To fulfill my dream, I thought I needed someone else to give me permission, approval, or the green light.

If you have your own version of this going on, wanting your partner, parents, friends, boss, or coworkers to approve of you or save you, this is something to celebrate because it's clearly pointing to some confusion you have around who you actually are. And if you have confusion, it means you've pulled a veil over your power. The good news is if it's a veil that was placed on you, often unconsciously, it can also be unfurled, tossed, and fed to the fire. In preparation for letting this pattern go, take a deep breath and let yourself go deep into today's video diary. Remember to stay curious. You won't know the deeper answer until you start speaking, like a child digging for treasure in the wild.

Today's Video Diary Prompt ☑

If I fully own my power and worth, I'm afraid that ...

Day 11

Bleeding Heart Block

We have to learn to let the chips fall where they may,
especially when they're not our f*ing chips!
—Terri Cole

Many of the clients and students I work with fear saying the wrong thing, unintentionally offending someone, or getting criticized for what comes out of their mouths. Because I work with empaths, healers, and coaches who want to make others feel good, they subconsciously hold themselves back to avoid mistakenly making people feel bad by shining too brightly or saying the wrong thing. This over-responsibility for others is associated with one of the seven core visibility blocks that I refer to as the Bleeding Heart Block. The Bleeding Heart Block keeps many empaths and highly sensitive people hiding to avoid discomfort, theirs or someone else's. Although it may seem pure, it actually stems from fear.

The Bleeding Heart Block is at work when you have so much empathy and sensitivity that you withhold parts of yourself because you don't want to hurt anyone. When this block is running, you feel the whole world's pain, which results in your being overly careful about sharing anything that might be difficult or confronting for somebody to hear.

Another way of thinking of this block is being locked in the people-pleasing good-girl cage. If you sacrifice your truth to avoid conflict, if you silence what you really want to say so that nobody's feathers are ruffled, or you find that you're constantly walking on eggshells, assessing how other people are digesting you and your message, the Bleeding Heart Block is very likely active.

Silencing our valuable voices is a painful way of living because we as empaths are here to be Leaders of Love, not followers of fear. If you fear your full-blast self, are hypervigilant about other people's emotional states, psychically trespass by trying to figure out what others are thinking of you, and shrink to keep the peace, this is likely a trauma response from childhood that kept you safe. You came into this world shining as brightly as a lighthouse and got trained into being a sponge, absorbing everyone else's energy. The good news is that you don't need to walk around absorbing and chronically temperature-checking other people's energy as an adult who is being called to stand in her true power.

I personally know the pain of the Bleeding Heart Block after decades of basing my okay-ness on whether or not others were okay. It's taken me a long time to understand that other people's triggers are not my responsibility and that walking on eggshells is not living. It's a way of worshipping fear and holding the middle finger up to love. Sorry to put it so bluntly, but it's true. Holding back may create so-called peace on the outside, but it hurts on the inside because love is here to be shared, not contained.

I often say to my community, if others have to wear sunglasses to look at you, so be it! That's their job. Your job is to be you— shine! You probably don't fit into the norm because you were born to stand out and help birth a new, healthier reality in our world. If we hold back, we're going against ourselves. Let yourself receive what you need to feel stable and thrive as you serve your message!

The Bleeding Heart Block is like an open wound that makes one feel too vulnerable to stand tall. This is an identity issue. You think you're the wound. The good news is that you're not the wound. You're the light that enters the wound, the mother who embraces the child, the lover who tenderly holds the places inside that hurt, which you'll get a felt sense for in upcoming chapters.

I work with a lot of bleeding hearts. I understand them because I was one and am a recovering people-pleaser myself. This block is a courage problem and eclipses the heart chakra. Yes, however incomprehensible this may seem to some empaths, feeling and caring too much is an obstacle to love. It's codependency wrapped in a *holier-than-thou* garment. It may feel like worrying and overextending oneself is love, but it's not. It's a control pattern. It's a trauma response to feeling unsafe, likely in childhood. Many of us had a bully, emotionally imbalanced parent, or narcissist as one of our caregivers, so we learned to people-please to stay safe. I remember as a little girl being able to dismantle someone's rage by gushing praise and putting on a smile that lit up the room. People-pleasing was my superpower … until it overstayed its welcome and began eating me up inside, eventually leading to a health diagnosis.

Many empaths take pride in caring to the point of rumination because they believe it makes them good. Excessively caring actually holds many of us back. This may be a lot to swallow. This was hard for me too when I started to consider my niceness as a disease that was hurting me rather than a trophy that made me worth something.

Don't take my word for it.

Simply ask yourself: How is taking on the weight of the world's suffering going for you? Is it helping you shine or is it bringing you down?

I remember my ex-partner, Jason, who is one of my greatest teachers, continuously schooling me on how to stop generating unnecessary suffering for myself. We once walked by a dead bird and I fell dark, a *woe is me* story swallowing me whole as the back of my hand pressed to my forehead on the way down. He had us stand together by the bird to say a Sanskrit prayer, as he encouraged me to stay neutral. At first, it seemed impossible and heartless. Eventually, I learned to see what was in front of me as it was without layering a story on top. I was finding the power of equanimity. The energetic payoff was huge as I chose to see, stay present, and be neutral through life's daily ups and downs. I was stepping into a new possibility where I could keep my energy for myself and have so much more to give because I wasn't being dragged down by what I call the *savior slump*.

What I discovered is that you can't worry enough to help others find peace. You can't be broke enough to give money to the poor. You can't be sick enough to empower people to heal. And you certainly can't feel enough pity to bring a bird back to life. I used to try to help others by jumping into the ditch with them until I realized I had to be out of the ditch to lend a hand.

If you were the peacekeeper in your family growing up, or you faced any kind of bullying in your childhood, then you likely have the Bleeding Heart Block running. It's a very painful block to be stuck behind, because when you're overly responsible for other people's feelings, you become a prisoner of overthinking, incapable of just being yourself and enjoying your life.

If you want to share a valuable message that helps others, there's an even bigger problem with the Bleeding Heart Block. When you hold back your authenticity and water down your message, you become invisible. By trying to appeal to everyone, you reach no one. Your message turns tepid.

Have you ever seen the first few seconds of a video and thought, *That's sweet, that's nice,* as you clicked away? The last thing you're going to do is invest in one of their programs or continue watching their content. Why? Because you can energetically feel they don't have the courage to speak the truth or offer anything other than a mash-up of what's popular and widely accepted. At best, you'll watch some things here and there, but you're not going to work with them because they're not in their authority, they're not in their authenticity. There's no clear perspective to gain value from. So, you keep scrolling. Next!

One way this block can limit empath entrepreneurs especially is through a resistance to making paid offers or promoting your services because you don't want to be seen as pushy. I used to have this block like the best of the bleeding hearts. It's important to get rid of this if you want to make money helping others.

I'll never forget my first business coach in 2017 instructing me to write an email that contained a teachable moment followed by a clear paid offer, and blast it to my community. I felt sick to my stomach. I didn't want to come off as pushy, slimy, or salesy. I knew it was the next right step for me to break through into greater impact and income. I'd been sending lots of free value, but avoided voicing my paid offers at all costs—at the cost of myself! Knowing it was what I needed to do didn't make it any easier, however.

Somehow, I mustered up the courage after taking hours writing the email, and I hit SEND. *Gulp!* I covered my mouth as I darted from my chair to lay on the couch. I was overtaken by nausea. In hindsight, in that distressing moment I was breaking through the Bleeding Heart Block by being boldly myself, sharing my powerful message, inviting people to pay to work with me, and letting them handle themselves and their interpretations of me. That one act thrust me into freedom as I got present with my queasy stomach, tenderly breathed through it, and celebrated myself for my courage.

There's something important I want you to understand when it comes to the Bleeding Heart Block that many coaches, healers, and spiritual teachers who are struggling to enroll clients and students don't realize:

People might think you're sweet and nice, but they'll click away and you'll wonder, *Why do I keep getting crickets when what I want are clients? Why are people finding me but not subscribing or buying my programs? Why can't people see me?!*

It's because you become invisible in the process of chronically attempting to please everyone and *good girl* your way to safety.

Pleasing others and burying your authenticity is like an eraser that deletes you from the scene. Your voice becomes like elevator music playing in the background that no one notices and everyone talks over. You become invisible when you play good.

After hitting burnout, getting a health diagnosis, and facing a massive wall in my relationship, I collapsed on a call with my therapist and mentor. I barely got the words out through my guttural weeping and gasping, "I'm—so—tired—of—being—goooood!"

I'll never forget his response.

BAM! POOF! WHAT?!

My jaw dropped, the tears stopped, and the grip on my throat released in an instant. It never occurred to me that my job wasn't to be a people-pleasing good girl who earned her worth through saving others from pain at the cost of her own. It was a life-changing moment for me because it woke me up to what I needed to know and live: My job is not to please others, but to be myself wholly and completely.

Today's Video Diary Prompt

The thing I'd say publicly if I didn't worry about offending anyone is …

Day 12

Persecution Wound

They tried to bury us, but they didn't know we were seeds.
—Mexican Proverb

Visibility blocks aren't just about hiding your face; they're about quieting your voice before anyone has the chance to hear you. Each of the seven visibility blocks limit your ability to express yourself freely. But one block, centered in the throat chakra, directly impacts your ability to speak your truth with confidence. This block is called the Persecution Wound and is common amongst empaths, highly sensitive people, healers, and those who see better ways of living for humanity, and want to help others find them.

Some refer to this block as the Witch Wound. Ultimately, this block is the result of a collective trauma carried generationally through our ancestors. The Persecution Wound was formed and has been reinforced throughout history when spiritually minded people expressed their intuitive or healing gifts and were met with violence. There are countless examples of spiritually oriented people being faced with danger, even persecution and death as a result. The Persecution Wound isn't something to dismiss or sweep away. It's real, and for many of us, a silent cellular injury is running unconsciously, keeping us from feeling safe when it comes to being seen. Whether you believe in ancestral trauma or past lives is irrelevant. What matters here is that we're all part of the same human family. Our history can dictate our destiny if we don't learn from it and release ourselves from its limits so we can rescript our lives in an empowered way.

History shows that if we don't heal things from the past, they carry through our lineage. Due to the Persecution Wound, there can be a very deep fear that if I express my feminine, healing gifts, I am going to be hurt or harmed. One way of determining if you have this visibility block is when you know you have an important message to share, but you find it difficult to get the words out. You may have this substantive body of work brewing inside, but it feels too big to capture and express. You may not know where to start with sharing your message because it feels ungraspable.

People with this block often have a clear connection to the unseen, or a brilliant idea and vision of what they want to create in this world. However, with the Persecution Wound present, you likely feel confused because the path forward is blurred, making it impossible to take a step. This can be a sign that you're connected to ancient wisdom that you're called to share, but there's fear obscuring it to keep you quiet. Confusion is one of the ways the unconscious will work to keep you out of harm's way. If you don't know what to say or how to move forward, you'll stay where you are. This is a temporary relief for a battered nervous system, but in the long run, it perpetuates the pain of playing small until you know how to regulate your nervous system, which we'll get to.

If you often feel tension in your throat, like you swallowed a frog, a choking sensation, the Persecution Wound is likely the cause. Have you ever had the experience of not being able to get the words out fast enough? Maybe it's difficult or seemingly impossible to express yourself? You may even feel an energetic strangling sensation in your throat chakra. Another common sign of the Persecution Wound is not knowing where to start with sharing your voice because your wisdom feels vague or too vast. You may struggle with how to break down your ideas into digestible, concrete, and shareable bits for a presentation, for example.

I went through this for years during a growth spurt in my business. I'd sit with my partner to put a curriculum together, and my ideas would bundle up in the back of my throat, unable to get out. I'd come to the table with my notes. I was on fire with pages of content, after days of spontaneous downloads and brilliant ideas that often came during meditation. But, when I went to speak them out loud to him, it felt like someone was strangling me and forcing me to stay silent. It was aggravating to feel so alive and clear about what I'm here to express, but my throat would aggressively constrict, slowing me down until I came to a complete stop.

The wisdom and creativity inside of me felt like a roaring river trying to move through a straw. I remember looking at him on several occasions while holding my throat, trying to understand what was happening. Eventually, I had a session with a healer for something unrelated and he told me about a horrific past life when I was a renowned spiritual teacher who was tortured and killed in a devastating way. It was so gruesome that I wouldn't dare share it here. When he told me, even though I'm not a firm believer in past lives, I gushed a tsunami of tears. Something dark and heavy spontaneously lifted from my soul. It's something I'll never forget. It gave me so much compassion for the protective mechanism within me that wanted me quiet, small, and unnoticeable.

If you keep your spiritual side in the closet and have extreme resistance to getting on camera, being visible, and sharing your voice, you're probably carrying this wound or you're bound by the collective pain of this wound. If your throat has ever closed up when you tried to say something in front of a group or your mind scattered into confusion, this may stem from the terror of being persecuted for speaking up. If you think, *I just don't know where to start* or you dread the idea of losing your train of thought in front of people, this block is likely going on for you. Deep down, there may be a fear of losing a sense of stability or control, sounding crazy, and being persecuted for it.

I know this can sound extreme if you haven't investigated why your throat chakra shuts down or you lose your voice when you try to speak in front of a group. However, if you study the Inquisition, exterminations of indigenous healers or countless other examples of light bringers and way-showers being killed, often hanged, for saying something counter to authority figures, you may find yourself sighing with compassion. We humans carry mountains of collective fear from being punished for authentic expression, which is why it's so important to heal our visibility blocks, establish calm in our nervous systems, and energetically disrupt the cycle.

We're all connected to each other, to the collective. Traumatic historical events are written into our DNA. For generations, people have been persecuted for radiating love, owning their intuition, or carrying spiritual wisdom the world wasn't ready to receive. So, on a subconscious level, we may carry a direct blockage or distortion due to collective trauma that can hold the expression of our deeper gifts hostage.

The good news is that there are also countless heroic examples of courageous souls speaking up and triumphing over collective hate, which is also written into our DNA. You choosing to clear your visibility blocks and share what's signed on your heart makes you the good news and can help tip the scale toward humanity's wholeness.

You are the good news!

You can clear your visibility blocks and as a result potentially contribute to the strengthening and evolution of the human spirit by sharing what your heart knows and loves.

Today's Video Diary Prompt

If the block in my throat chakra could speak, it would say …

Day 13

Comparison Cage

*The primary cause of unhappiness is never the situation but
your thoughts about it. Be aware of the thoughts you are
thinking. Separate them from the situation,
which is always neutral. It is as it is.*
—Eckhart Tolle

oday, we're exploring the core block that lives in the sixth
chakra or *third eye*, which I call the Comparison Cage.

Yes—*a cage.*

You may know it well. It shows up as the voice that whispers,
Why bother? Someone's already doing it … and doing it better. It's
what keeps you watching from the sidelines, seeing others say
the very things you're passionate about, while you hold back.
You hesitate. You tell yourself the space is already full. That your
message has already been said. That others are more confident,
more qualified, more charismatic, more *capable*.

And so, you don't speak.

You don't share.

You scroll, compare, judge, admire, analyze, rinse and
repeat, … but you don't show up.

For some, it's a quiet sense of not-enoughness. For others, it turns outward—maybe you feel frustrated, even agitated by what others are saying. You see messages that feel off or misaligned, and a fire rises in you because you want to offer a different perspective. But even with that fire, you stay quiet. You still hold it in.

That's the Comparison Cage in action.

It tricks you into thinking you're being cautious, humble, or discerning. But underneath all of it is one sticky, familiar emotion: fear. Specifically, this fearful block originates in the third visibility block of not being good enough. The Comparison Cage and Not Enough Trance are often linked, like overbearing sisters trying to keep you safe in the best way they know how.

Sometimes it's obvious. Sometimes it's subtle. But if you're not sharing your voice in the way you long to, comparison is almost always playing a role.

And here's what makes this cage especially tricky: It looks so reasonable. It dresses up like logic. You might say things like:

- "There's no room for me in this space."
- "They've already said it so beautifully."
- "I don't have anything new to add."
- "I'm not ready yet."

But these thoughts are often just fear pretending to be logic—fear that stems from deeply internalized ideas about worth, visibility, and safety.

And for empaths and sensitives, this fear hits hard. We feel so much. We notice everything. And that sensitivity, if not honored and understood, can keep us locked in self-protection mode.

So we stay quiet. We dim. We delay.

We watch others live the very vision we dream of ... and bury our own potential.

But deep down, we know the truth: *We want to be out there too.*

We want to be seen. We want to share what's in our hearts. We want to speak.

And yet, something holds us back.

That's the Comparison Cage.

And the wildest part? Many of us don't even know we're in it.

One of my clients—a relationship coach—despite everything she had to offer, kept running up against the Comparison Cage and all-consuming bouts of self-doubt.

She had a story that could move mountains. Her wisdom was born from the fire of her own transformation. Not something she read in a book—something she *lived through.* But still, she couldn't quite bring herself to share it fully and consistently show up. Not because it wasn't valuable. But because she was caught in the Comparison Cage.

Her days became a spin cycle of watching. Other coaches. Their courses. Their content. She studied them like sacred texts. And with every scroll, with every module ... she felt smaller.

Self-doubt was swallowing her. She didn't realize it then, but she was feeding the story that said: *They've got it. I don't. They're clearer. Smarter. More credible.*

It wasn't inspiration—it was paralysis.

In my membership during one of our coaching calls, she asked me if she should change her content. She'd just taken a successful relationship coach's course, and their method *really* worked. But this method wasn't natural to her, nor from her lived experience. "Would I be a fraud?" she asked. "Or should I just do it because it's what people seem to want?"

But this wasn't about a content strategy. It was about her worth.

We peeled back the layers. And there it was—tears. Not from sadness, but from seeing what was happening inside herself deep down.

She could *see* the pattern now. How she was using comparison as a shield. To stay small. To avoid standing in her power. To stay safe. To keep self-doubt as her master.

Because sometimes, your nervous system clings to the discomfort it knows. And for her, that discomfort was feeling *not good enough.* Comparison wasn't just a habit. It was so familiar that it felt like home.

But that moment cracked something open. She saw how much of her own wisdom she was swallowing. How much gold she was sitting on. How the world wasn't asking her to *borrow* someone else's brilliance, but to bring her own.

And that was the beginning.

The Comparison Cage doesn't dissolve overnight. But when you see it for what it is—not truth, but protection of a false you—you can insert the key to unlock the door. And take your first step into your visibility—your voice, your authentic way.

I'll show you how she did it—and how you can too—in the next section.

For now, keep in mind that many of us have normalized the inner monologue of comparison so much, we think it's just being *realistic*. But the truth is, it's keeping us small. It's keeping our voices quiet. And it's slowly draining the joy out of what we're here to do.

So today, instead of rushing to fix it, let's just name it. Let's be honest about where it's showing up.

Let's turn inward with compassion and curiosity—and look at where this block might be quietly shaping our choices, driving our silence, and limiting our self-perception.

Because the first step in any transformation is awareness.

Today's Video Diary Prompt

The person I'm most envious of or agitated by is _____ because …

Use this prompt not to judge yourself, but to get honest. Let this be a mirror. Often, envy, frustration, or agitation are arrows pointing us to a truth we've buried, a desire we've denied, or a part of ourselves that's ready to rise.

Perfectionist Headlock

Perfectionism is not a way to avoid shame.
Perfectionism is a form of shame.
—Brené Brown

Today, we're taking a look at the seventh and final core visibility block that, when left unaddressed, can lead to a painful cycle of procrastination and endless deferring of your dreams. I call it the Perfectionist Headlock.

Think of this as the crown of your chakra system—the part of your energetic body that connects you to divine vision and purpose. But when perfectionism takes over, instead of being open and expansive, it's like having your head caught in a chokehold. And I don't say that lightly. I've lived this one, deeply. It actually *feels* like a headlock when the perfectionist is in charge—tight, relentless, and suffocating.

You might be in the grip of it if you keep putting off your creative work—the post, the podcast, the video, the offer, the program—telling yourself you'll do it *once it's perfect*. That you'll speak once you've refined the message. Share your story when your website is polished. Go live after you buy the fancy mic and find a flattering light. You might even be hearing that sneaky voice say, *I just need one more certification*, or *I don't look good enough on camera,* or *My voice sounds weird when I talk*. I've had clients scrutinize themselves so closely that they say things like, "I don't like the way my nose moves when I speak," or "I look awkward," or "My branding isn't ready yet."

Sound familiar?

These are *not* facts. These are perfectionist thoughts—and they create a kind of mental headlock that will keep you circling the runway, never quite taking off. The painful part is that while all of this is happening in your mind, your deeper self *knows* you're ready. You feel it. The longing is there. But the headlock tightens every time you get close.

It's painful because you *know* there's something important inside you—something meaningful you want to express, something that wants to be shared. And yet … you wait. You stall. You tweak. You overthink. You look around at people doing what you want to be doing and tell yourself, *One day, when I've got it just right.*

I faced this block head-on in an unexpected way while writing this book. Once we get to the solution in the next section, I'll share more on that and the deeper insight I gained.

For now, let me gently offer this: *Perfectionism is a liar.* A seductive one. It says, *Once you've got this all figured out, then you can begin.* But it's a lie. Because even when you hit that imaginary milestone of *ready*, it will move the goalpost again. And again. And again.

There's a particular flavor of this block that I call Superstar Syndrome. It shows up when you only want to share your voice if you're *certain* it'll be the best. You want the gold star, the applause, the flawless delivery. If you can't be spectacular, you won't even start. This usually goes all the way back to childhood—where maybe you received praise, love, or attention only when you were exceptional. So somewhere along the line, a belief was formed: *If I'm not the best, I won't be accepted. If I'm not perfect, I won't be loved.* It's deep. It's old. And it's a thief. It steals dreams and stashes them in some fairy-tale future that never arrives.

If you're a chronic overthinker who goes into analysis paralysis, ruminating over what you want to create, but never going for it—that's the headlock. If you can't bear the thought of being *just okay* at something, if you're afraid of looking silly or ordinary, if your self-worth is riding on your performance, welcome to the club. This is the perfectionist steering the ship.

Don't get me wrong, being dedicated to excellence is a beautiful thing. But, let's be real for a second: Perfectionism is painful, it edges the joy out of life. Instead of being a free-spirited child happily smearing paint across a canvas with your bare hands, you get praised for being the one who *has it all together,* coloring precisely between the lines. It can look shiny and impressive on the outside. But behind the scenes it's isolating.

There's nothing glamorous about camouflaged terror. Because that's what perfectionism is—*fear in a fancy dress* (shout-out to Julia Cameron, author of *The Artist's Way,* for that gem). It's fear that's been accessorized to look like ambition. But underneath the polish is panic.

Sometimes, the perfectionist's grip doesn't keep us invisible—it just keeps us exhausted. I know this firsthand. I was fully visible—teaching self-care, helping coaches raise their frequency, guiding them into confidence. On the outside, it looked like I had it all together. But behind the scenes I was burning myself out trying to make everything *perfect.*

I'd spend hours preparing for a single live class—writing, rewriting, organizing index cards. Two hours in hair and makeup just to feel *ready.* It was intense. Not because I didn't know my stuff, but because I felt like I had to hold it all together, give value at the highest level, and look like Cindy Crawford doing it. Yeah, good luck with that!

Meanwhile, my partner Jason would spend his prep time in meditation. Three hours, deep in stillness. Then he'd toss on a hat, grab a nice shirt, sit down, and trust whatever wanted to come through. His hair wild under that hat, no notes, no pressure. Just presence. And you know what? It worked. People loved his transmission. He led with energy, not effort.

I remember looking at my hands minutes before going live—literally shaking. The weight of pressure on my shoulders was crushing. And while my content always landed, it came at a cost. For them, it was high value. For me, it was self-abandonment.

Eventually, my body said it'd had enough. I was diagnosed with a confronting illness. Perfectionism had turned into a silent war inside me. The outbursts, the frustration, the emotional fatigue—all signs I wasn't being true to myself.

Jason showed me another way. He honored his state of consciousness first. He trusted that what wanted to come through him would. That was the difference.

This block lives in the crown chakra. When perfectionism is running the show, there's limited space for divine wisdom to flow. You can create success from that space, sure. But when it's fueled by force, the one person who doesn't win is you.

If you've been holding yourself to an impossible standard … If you've been waiting until your voice is smooth, your message is refined, your following is massive … If you've been putting off visibility until it's certain you'll never mess up or be misunderstood, or you are visible but harming yourself in the grip of perfectionism …

Then this is your invitation to take the fancy dress off. Let yourself get a little messy. Be real. Be seen as *you are*—not as some curated version of yourself. This is the beginning of returning to your authentic self. The version of you that came into this world open, expressive, and unfiltered—before you learned to perform, perfect, and collect gold stars for getting it right.

We'll get into how to untangle this Perfectionist Headlock later. But for now, I'm inviting you to pause and reflect.

Are you willing to feel safe being visible *without* being perfect? Can you imagine letting go of the pressure to impress and simply being *real*? Are you open to discovering a kind of confidence that remains steady, even when you flop?

The fact that you're reading this book tells me something important—you're already saying yes. So congratulations. You're further along than you think.

Today's Video Diary Prompt ☑

The first person I remember trying to be perfect for was _____ because …

Phase III

SEVEN FACETS OF CONFIDENT VISIBILITY

Becoming Your Own Safety

When we fight with our failings,
we ignore the entrance to the shrine itself.
—David Whyte

Welcome to phase 3 of our journey—where we begin to unlock the solutions to all seven core visibility blocks, starting with the first: the antidote to the Vow of Smallness. This particular block is rooted in the base chakra and often wears the mask of mediocrity. But here's the deeper truth: Many of us didn't dim our light because we lacked potential—we dimmed it because we were ignored, punished, or made to feel unsafe for simply being ourselves. For shining too brightly. For being different. For taking up space.

To unravel the false belief that staying small keeps us safe, we must begin with a powerful shift: *learning to become our own source of safety.*

This isn't a poetic suggestion. It's a nervous-system imperative. Visibility naturally stirs up old insecurities, often rooted in childhood. So if your younger self learned that standing out invites harm, she'll continue to choose hiding, even if your adult self is ready to be seen.

Becoming your own safety means making a sacred pivot—from sourcing your sense of worth from others, to becoming your own source of validation and love. This requires grounding into your body so that you can be a fierce guardian of your energy and the inner child that is still very much alive energetically within us all, no matter what age we are. If the term *inner child* doesn't resonate with you, then you can get creative and use different terminology.

And here's the catch: You can't think your way into safety. You get to *feel* your way there.

Why Overthinking Feels Safe—But Isn't

One of the most normalized but toxic patterns we've inherited is overthinking. Worry doesn't solve problems—it creates stress, exhausts our bodies, and keeps our nervous systems in a state of defense. When we're locked in our minds, we abandon the one place we can actually feel safe: our bodies.

When you're about to make a video, speak on stage, or even send a vulnerable email, if you're overthinking—trying to see yourself through everyone else's eyes—you're not grounded in your body. You're not centered in your heart. You've left yourself. This is a subtle way of abandoning ourselves and our bodies. And the body knows it. It tightens, trembles, or grows numb.

Years ago, I filmed executive coaches—brilliant, accomplished leaders—and the moment the camera came on, many of them visibly shrank. They lost their words, broke out in stress rashes, or performed inauthentically. It wasn't a lack of skill. It was a nervous system unprepared to be seen.

That's why visibility work doesn't start with performance techniques. It begins with nervous system regulation and becoming your own safety so you feel grounded and centered.

The ONE Method:
A Practice to Anchor You

To help you become your own safety, I created the ONE Method—a three-step embodiment practice for calming your nervous system and reclaiming your center before you create, share, or voice your message so that it can move others.

Step 1: Offer Yourself an Embrace

Place one hand on your heart, one on your belly. Say to yourself: *I'm here with you, and I'm not leaving.*

This may seem simple, but to your mammalian nervous system, physical touch equals safety. It sends the signal: *You're not alone, you're not in danger.*

Rub your hands together to warm them first if you'd like. Then hold yourself like a loving mother would a frightened child.

This isn't about indulging fear—it's about *meeting* it. When you embrace yourself, you become the one who holds the scared part of you instead of being identified as the fear.

Step 2: Neutralize Your Nervous System with Balance Breathing

Breathe slowly. Inhale through your nose—first into the belly, then bring your breath up to your heart space.

Pause.

Exhale through your mouth—slowly.

Pause.

Keeping your hands on your body, repeat this cycle for 10 slow breaths or for 2 minutes … 120 seconds of pure self-love! Let your breath carry you from the noise of your thoughts down into the safety of your body. This is balance. This is presence. This slow, steady breathing pattern sends signals of safety to your nervous system.

Step 3: **E**xpress Yourself Freely

Before recording a video or speaking, try what I call a Wild Child Warm-up: stomp your feet, shake your body, growl or roar—yes, really. This is your chance to howl at the moon!

Stomping your feet declares *I am here, and I have the right to be here.* This is especially important for empaths who have been told blatantly or subtly that they're too much. To be quiet.

If you feel safe, accustomed to, or even valued for people-pleasing your way through life by putting others first, this will be a necessary practice for you.

Roaring declares that I have a voice and I'm setting it free. I'm no longer willing to stifle it behind a whisper, etiquette, or *good-girling*.

The Wild Child Warm-up, especially stomping, activates the first chakra, grounding you into your body. Simply stomp, shake out your body (including your head), or do a tribal dance if you'd like. The key is to move, hop into your body, and stomp! Left foot, right foot! Stomp! Stomp! Stomp!

Try it. Take up space. Let the shy, silent part of you *move* and then *speak* without editing. Explore: *If I could say anything right now, I'd say ... What I'm feeling right now is ...*

Anything goes!

Do this privately. Just for your eyes. It's not about polish. It's about presence. You'll be delighted by how much more energized and real your videos or conversations feel afterward. You'll shift from *performing* to *speaking from presence*—and people can feel the difference. Most importantly, *you'll* feel the difference.

For years, I did the Wild Child Warm-up before videos, and what would come out of me sometimes sounded like: *I don't want to make this video. I have nothing to say. I could give a sh*beeeeep what you think of me, ya ding-dong. Arghhh!! I'm tired of having to perform, look pretty, and play perfect.* I had so much pent-up anger for all the years I portrayed a flawless image on stages, starting as young as four years old walking the runway in department stores.

The Wild Child Warm-up helped me find my authenticity. I'd roar, ululate, and laugh myself into vibrant energy and confidence, using that energy to feed even more life into my meaningful message. Before I embraced this, my expression was tight and measured, dulled by perfectionism's grip.

I discovered this practice while on the Mendocino coast in California during a transformational period of living in solitude in the redwoods. I write about this in my first book, *The Diamond Process™*. The waves were so loud that my roars faded in. Something about the intense wind and fog, the rawness of the land, helped me free the wild woman I had pent up inside of me. It felt like heaven to scream like hell. This kind of raw, unfiltered expression was a powerful catalyst in my healing—and a turning point on my path to confidence. That was right around the time I started making videos on YouTube.

What Makes The ONE Method Transformative

The ONE Method works because it centers you in your body—your home—rather than in your mind, which can so easily turn against you.

The moment you feel safe with yourself, you become unshakable. Not because the fear disappears, but because you're no longer outsourcing your safety to how others perceive you.

You reclaim your power. You stop shrinking. You stop hiding.

You stop being the thief of your valuable message and instead feel the glee of setting it free.

Saying a Sweet Goodbye to Smallness

You can be doing all the *right* things—posting, creating, building a business—but if your body doesn't feel safe, you'll sabotage yourself or stop. You'll hide after one burst of visibility. Or find reasons to stay in the background.

The solution is not more hustle. It's more safety. More breath. More self-trust.

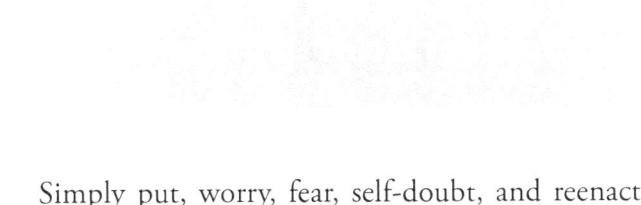

Simply put, worry, fear, self-doubt, and reenacting events in our minds tends to be the default setting for most people. All that does is keep one small. One of the greatest addictions in modern culture is overthinking. There's nothing safe, stabilizing, or sane about overthinking, yet most of us do it much of the time! This isn't something to judge yourself for—that would strengthen overthinking. Hopefully, this brings you compassion and provokes your commitment to replace the danger signals that overthinking sends the body, to becoming your own safety instead. With every moment you stay present—tuning in to your body, breathing deeply, and expressing your truth authentically through the ONE Method for just 120 seconds—you're gently writing a farewell letter to smallness, and embodying the radiant lighthouse you were created to be.

When you root yourself in your body and become your own sanctuary, you build a steady foundation of calm and confidence essential for being a Visible Empath. This isn't a one-time act—it's a daily practice. Just 120 seconds a day of this simple ritual can transform your life.

Today's Video Diary Prompt

Ask yourself:
What emotion does my body feel in this moment? (Name it)
Where do I feel it? (Locate it)
If this emotion could speak safely, without judgment, what would it say?
And let it speak.
Let yourself be compassionately witnessed—by you.

Day 16

How to Regulate Your Emotions

Perhaps all the dragons in our lives are princesses who
are only waiting to see us act, just once, with beauty and
courage. Perhaps everything that frightens us is, in its deepest
essence, something helpless that wants our love.
—Rainer Maria Rilke

et's explore the second core visibility block that keeps so many empaths spinning in motion but stuck in place: The Busy Bee Block.

As we touched on in day 9, this block doesn't always look like fear—it often disguises itself as noble busyness. It shows up as packed calendars, overflowing to-do lists, and a constant sense of being too overwhelmed or overextended to focus on the thing your soul is quietly—or loudly—calling you toward.

You may find yourself constantly going—moving, doing, tending to everything and everyone, while your truest desires—your message, your creativity, your visibility—wait patiently on the back burner for *the right time.*

And let's be honest: That time never comes.

Here's a truth worth repeating—this block isn't actually about your calendar or not having enough time. It's about intimacy. Emotional intimacy with yourself.

This is an avoidance pattern. The Busy Bee stays busy not just out of habit, but because slowing down would mean feeling things. And feeling things—especially the uncomfortable emotions like fear, grief, anger, hurt, longing, or rejection—can seem unbearable when we haven't yet learned how to be with them in a loving, effective way. These repressed feelings can even manifest as inflammation and pain in the body, adding fuel to the attempt to flee discomfort.

You might *talk* about your feelings but never actually *feel* them. If you're constantly in your head—reading, researching, planning, learning, checking boxes, and consuming more content than you create—it may be a sign that you're unconsciously running from your own emotional body and the fear-driven thoughts that feed pain. If feeling uncomfortable emotions scares you, please take a breath. This is normal. Most of us never learned how to effectively manage our thoughts and feelings. This means there is a wonderful opportunity to become aware and curious about the deeper *why* behind your commitment to avoid valid feelings that are buried inside. Once you know what you're truly afraid of, you can bring safety and solutions in. You may also consider working with a professional therapist or somatic healer to help you consciously feel what you feel.

Just as the first block, the Vow of Smallness, invites us to become our own safety by returning to and embracing the physical body, the Busy Bee Block calls us into an equally sacred task: to become a warm, compassionate presence for our emotional self, especially the insecure aspects. This is how we begin to root into unshakable confidence.

Not by doing more or thinking about what we're feeling. But by feeling our feelings rather than fleeing them.

I won't lie to you: This practice of emotional intimacy can be confronting at first. But it's also the doorway to your freedom. The more intimate you become with your feelings, the more powerful and magnetic your visibility becomes.

So, take a deep breath with me. Light a candle, if you'd like. Let this be a sacred moment—an invitation to come home to yourself.

Inhale deeply

And exhale slowly.

Soften the jaw. Relax your brow and belly.

Let yourself *land*.

Let's gently step into a short practice together. This is a foundational exercise that can help clear the Busy Bee Block and bring you back to the steady, powerful rhythm of your own truth.

The Emotional Spotlight Practice

Place one hand on your belly and one hand on your heart.

Close your eyes as you exhale.

Breathe into the space between your hands. This simple act begins to lower cortisol and invites your nervous system to soften.

Four Questions to Embody Calm Using the Emotional Spotlight Practice

Ask yourself:

- 1. **What am I feeling right now?**
  Name it. Without judgment. It might be anxiety, bliss, grief, peace, frustration. Name the feeling that is present. If you have trouble identifying what you feel, simply choose from one of the four primary emotions: anger, fear, joy, sadness.
- 2. **Where do I feel it in my body?**
  Locate it. Maybe that tightness in your chest is grief. Maybe the flutter in your belly is excitement. Locate the feeling in your body. And breathe into it. If you feel the feeling in various places or all over, where do you feel it's the loudest? Once you locate the feeling, place your hands there and breathe.
- 3. **Am I willing to allow this feeling to exist?**
  You don't have to like the feeling. However, the resistance is what creates suffering. This is an opportunity to release

the habit of trying to fix or understand your feeling. Just let it be. Like a cloud passing through the sky. You are the sky. The feeling is simply weather. Like a mother whose small child storms into the room upset. You are not the child. You are the one who welcomes and holds the child as they feel what they feel.

- 4. **Ask the feeling directly: What do you need from me right now, sweetheart?**

  At the bottom of every strong feeling is usually an unmet need. So once you've named and located the emotion, it's important to ask what this feeling needs that it hasn't been getting. Sometimes the answer is *I need rest.* Sometimes it's *I need you to hold me.* Sometimes it's simply *I need to know I'm not wrong for feeling this way.* Honor what arises. Be gentle. If you need a good cry, let it come. If your teeth chatter, let them chatter. If a roar arises, let it blow the roof off. If all you can do is sit quietly and feel the breath in your belly, that's enough. It's plenty.

Many years ago, I was invited to speak at a theater in Los Angeles, where stories were being shared around a particular theme. The director gave me one clear directive: *Don't hold back.*

So I didn't. I shared my story—raw, vulnerable, unfiltered. I spoke the unspeakable: the childhood wounds, the misfortunes, the parts of my life I usually kept hidden behind a polished, capable exterior. I stood there, not performing for praise, but as a human being, choosing truth. Opting for honesty over image.

What I hadn't expected was how many people I knew would be in the audience. Among them was a woman who represented everything I used to put on a pedestal. She was beautiful, successful, poised—perfection incarnate. She sat in the front row, riveted.

And there I was, smashing the unblemished mask I had spent years varnishing.

On stage, I felt strong. Not fearless, but free. I had done it—I had shared my truth, not for approval, but to surrender the shame. And to serve. To help others heal through my story.

But offstage, something else surfaced.

One by one, people approached me with the same words: "You are so courageous." And instead of letting those words land as praise, I spiraled. I heard, "I can't believe you said that," or worse, "That was too much. *You* are too much!"

Old beliefs kicked in: *You overshared. You were messy. You failed to uphold the image.*

I went to sleep that night on a friend's blow-up mattress near the theater, drowning in a vulnerability hangover. My fearful ego was furious. *Why did you expose yourself? Why didn't you keep such unsexy truths silent?*

But this time, I didn't distract myself by planning or fixing or strategizing how to recover my image. I remembered my name: *Veronica*, the etymology of which means *true image*. The false image needed to fall.

Instead, as I lay in the dark like a mummy wrapped in a sleeping bag atop the inflatable bed, I asked: *What am I feeling? Where do I feel it?*

The answer: Worthlessness. Deep in my gut.

Am I willing to allow this feeling to exist? I devotedly placed my hands on my belly and breathed, not to get rid of it, but to be with it like I would with a malnourished orphan who has never known the feeling of being loved or chosen. I let the tears come. I approached slowly and carefully, holding that tender place inside instead of judging it or pushing it away. I didn't try to *do* anything—I simply *felt*. I asked the deeper question: *What is the unmet need here?*

The answer was simple: to be loved as I am.

Not once I *got it together*. Not once I looked powerful again. But now—raw, real, and imperfect.

And slowly, I found my footing in my grounded, present self—what I call the *Diamond Self* in my first book, *The Diamond Process™: Using Everyday Triggers to Awaken the Treasure Within.* I slept deeply that night, and woke up proud. Not because I had performed well, but because I had stayed with myself when it mattered most.

This is how we overcome the Busy Bee Block—not by doing more or proving our worth, but by feeling our feelings, meeting our needs, and embodying real confidence from the inside out.

This is how we begin to heal.

This is how we break the spell, the show of busyness that our culture applauds.

This is how we start showing up fully—without needing to escape, numb ourselves, or push away what's real.

This is how we release resistance around confidently going for our dreams and voicing our messages that move the world.

When feelings go unmet, they don't disappear. They lodge in the body. They wait. And they whisper things like, *You're not ready,* or *You don't have time,* or *You're too overwhelmed.*

When you become the kind, steady witness to your feelings, a present, compassionate *mother* to the tender places within—when you stop running—you become emotionally sovereign. You stop needing external conditions to be perfect before you can take a step forward or feel good about yourself because internally you feel safe.

And that's where confident visibility accelerates and the Confident Empath stands revealed.

So much of our insecurity around being visible is a fearful avoidance of being rejected or judged by others. This fear isn't coming from the adult, wise, empowered you. It's coming from a much earlier time, usually in childhood, when painful feelings were too big to feel, so we repressed them. These unfelt feelings got lodged in the nervous system as limiting beliefs, as blocks. And masks formed over them, locking the pain in place.

It can be helpful to imagine your feeling as a small child—maybe scared, hurt, or longing to be seen. Would you shut the door on them? Or would you open your arms, kneel down, and say, "Sweetheart, I see you. I've got you. You're not alone," as the child shakes or cries in your arms.

This is what your emotional body needs. And it's the beginning of true inner leadership. And consequently, strong outer leadership.

So if you've been caught in the loop of busyness, remember: The invitation isn't to hustle harder. It's to slow down and listen.

Let your feelings speak. Let your body guide you home to presence. And let presence become the unshakable foundation of your visibility, not to mention your life! This is how we use visibility as a path of spiritual awakening and liberating personal growth.

When you're no longer afraid to feel what you feel, no feedback, no comment, no rejection, no moment of imperfection can take you down.

You'll know how to stay with yourself. And that, my beautiful friend, is confidence that no one can give or take away.

Today's Video Diary Prompt ☑

What are you afraid of happening if you slow down?

Day 17

Own Your Worth and Unique Wisdom

Last night, as I was sleeping,
I dreamt—marvelous error!—
that I had a beehive
here inside my heart.
And the golden bees
were making white combs
and sweet honey
from my old failures.
—Antonio Machado

Today, you're being invited to take ownership of your personal power, wake up out of the Not Enough Trance, and stand tall in your worth.

As you now know from day 10, the Not Enough Trance is a common, unconscious program that sits in the third chakra, your energetic center of personal power. The Not Enough Trance says, *I'm not valuable enough. I'm not good enough. No matter what I do, I'll never be enough!* It's a painful lie to believe, and the good news is that the way through is simple.

In 2009, I was traveling the world first-class with the love of my life, whom I was contemplating marrying after nearly six incredible years together. I had the yoga body, was living in the lap of luxury, and had a deeply loving community of spiritual friends. I was living on purpose as my career was just starting to bloom as a transformational life coach. I was living a bright and shiny life by nearly anyone's standards, but inside I was stuck in darkness and turmoil.

My emotional suffering eventually became unbearable, so I left the life I'd built in Los Angeles and moved to the redwood forest alone to heal myself. I took all the yogic practices I was given in India, spiritual psychology tools I learned in my masters program, and every drop of wisdom the wise ones I sat with or read books by imparted, and I used them on myself. Mostly, though, I sat with the trees and learned how to love myself the way a safe, loving mother does.

It was a life-changing year in solitude. Spiritually, I was overflowing with riches, but when it came to the material world, I was practically penniless and felt worthless. Thoughts of the future filled me with anxiety, dread, and a sense of powerlessness. I knew I couldn't go back to a corporate job, nor a wealthy partner. I needed to find my own worth and create my own wealth by giving something of value to others, something that felt meaningful to my soul. This became clear while seated at my meditation space one afternoon, confessing how worthless and terrified I felt. Yes, I was speaking out loud by myself in an empty room. Some might call this crazy, but freely speaking the honest truths I'd been burying for decades beneath a deadening, perfect-looking mask became my lifeline.

Pressing my eyes closed, trails of tears falling from my face, I spontaneously saw an image in my mind's eye as I heard very clear inner guidance. I saw a book with my name on it. The four corners of the book really stood out to me, like the Four Directions in Native American tradition, indicating something solid, something real. *Veronica, you haven't gone through all of this to perpetually sit around crying and feeling powerless. It's time for you to take your wisdom and turn it into something tangible, something that can help people.* It was time to activate my valuable voice and stake my place in this world!

This was my light-switch moment. I went from feeling like I wasn't enough because of the balance in my bank account and no foreseeable way of changing it, to realizing that I was sitting on gold! I started to see that I was the heroine of my own life, of my own story, holding riches in the form of wisdom. And like any heroine in an epic story, I had goods to bring back to my community.

This vision gave me the strength to say goodbye to the redwoods, return to Los Angeles, reignite my coaching business, and take on three part-time jobs to make ends meet. Within nine months, I created my first online course, which later became my first book, *The Diamond Process™: Using Everyday Triggers to Awaken the Treasure Within,* and I left all of my part-time jobs. By no means was any of this easy, but because of my vision I had the power to move through every single obstacle and go for it. The rest is history!

I was pushed down by pain, and all it took was ONE holy instant to be pulled by vision—a vision that helped me see myself as a hero rather than a victim.

Many empaths and highly sensitive people fall into the Not Enough Trance—a state where they doubt their value because their expertise wasn't earned in traditional ways, or because they still face dark, messy moments and battle with imposter syndrome as a result. If this is you, congratulations—you're human! What you may not know is that your lived experiences *are* your wisdom. Those bathroom-floor moments are your doctorate credits. The pain you've alchemized into growth, the healing you've done, the insight you now carry—*this is your expertise.*

In one of my most popular programs, Confident Course Creation School™, I help clients unearth their expertise, what I call your Soul Signature Course. It's life-changing in the sense of igniting your sense of self-worth, purpose, and clarity of message. And it all starts with clarifying your story. Your transformational story is medicine for others who are struggling and who need to see living proof of someone like them who made it through to the other side. (We'll be mapping your story on day 24.) You can also go to https://www.thediamondprocess.com/story to get my free workshop, *Using Your Story to Help Others*.

When you own your voice and what you've lived through, you shift from self-doubt to service. Instead of asking, *Am I too much or not enough?* ask: *Who needs to hear this today?* When you show up from a place of service, your energy becomes magnetic.

I often encourage clients to keep an evidence journal—a space to collect client testimonials, breakthroughs, screenshots, and personal wins. This creates an instant pattern interrupt when self-doubt strikes. Flipping through proof of your impact helps quiet the inner critic on those darker days and reconnect you to your purpose.

Strengthening Your Third Chakra and Sense of Self-Worth

The Not Enough Trance is linked to the third chakra—your personal power center. When this is out of balance, it's hard to see your worth. That's why safety and emotional mastery are essential foundations before building visibility, which we explored in the previous two chapters. You must feel safe to be okay being seen and to have the audacity to own your worth and your wisdom.

This requires embracing your full messy magnificence. The parts you've tried to hide—your flaws, quirks, and vulnerable truths—often create the deepest connections. Too often, we filter our truth out of fear: *What will they think if they know I screw up sometimes?* But the very parts of you you've tried to hide can be the ley lines of deep connection between you and those you can help. Your struggles and *flaws* can become bridges of engagement and healing. And as you radically accept your humanness and flaws, especially the more insecure facets of yourself, you strengthen your self-worth.

One of the women in my membership, a self-love coach who is doing transformative work with clients, used to struggle with this. She'd share powerful, polished stories and then slip into *hustle and hide* patterns, going quiet after a launch, exhausted from upholding the perfect teacher image. Recently, she started dating again and shared a funny, unfiltered story in our Authenticity Circle in my membership. Everyone leaned in. Her messy, human moment lit up the space. If she included that version of herself in her business, sharing her stories as teachable gems, her audience would likely love her even more—because they'd feel more of her *realness and relatability*. And she'd stay energized, no longer draining herself hiding parts of who she is.

Living behind a mask is exhausting. I remember the late spiritual teacher, Debbie Ford, comparing it to holding a beach ball underwater, while you're smiling above water. The amount of energy that is required to push the ball down is enormous, leaving no room to relax and thrive. Of course being a professional is important. Aimlessly airing your dirty laundry is not the goal. However, true confidence comes from accepting the whole of yourself and showing up shamelessly. Sometimes that means using a real-life human story and teachable moment to help your clients, customers, and students.

If fear of being judged or rejected arises, remember: *Rejection means you're in the arena.* You've taken a stand for what counts rather than standing on the sidelines, like that quote from Teddy Roosevelt brings out:

> It is not the critic who counts: not the man who points out how the strong man stumbles or where the doer of deeds could have done better. The credit belongs to the man who is actually in the arena, whose face is marred by dust and sweat and blood, who strives valiantly, who errs and comes up short again and again, because there is no effort without error or shortcoming, but who knows the great enthusiasms, the great devotions, who spends himself for a worthy cause; who, at the best, knows, in the end, the triumph of high achievement, and who, at the worst, if he fails, at least he fails while daring greatly, so that his place shall never be with those cold and timid souls who knew neither victory nor defeat.

You're showing up, and that's powerful. Most people who criticize are not in the arena. They're the ones on the sidelines.

I've never met an empowered leader who criticized colleagues. Never. Not once. They may disagree on things, but they focus on creating their own value-driven content rather than trying to take someone down. I share this with you because taking directions from someone who has never been to where you're headed is not the best use of your time.

Fear of being seen often belongs to the inner child who once felt shamed for shining too brightly or stumbling in the spotlight. When you offer her safety, validation, and presence, visibility becomes natural. A regulated nervous system and consistent self-acknowledgment as you take brave action are what build lasting confidence—not perfection.

Remember, even 120 seconds a day of holding yourself into safety as you commit to being visible sharing your unique wisdom compounds into real momentum over time. **You don't need to be fearless—just *tender with yourself through the fears.*** This is how you rewire your nervous system for confidence—through presence, self-validation, and tiny, consistent acts of courage. Every time you speak your truth with love, you retrain your system to feel safe being seen. This is the heart of being a Visible Empath: embodying wholeness as you serve your message.

Pleasing isn't purpose; serving your valuable message is!

Own your expertise by owning the wisdom of your story.

Stand in your whole, human brilliance.

Your authenticity is your superpower—and there are people at this very moment who need what you've got!

Today's Video Diary Prompt ☑

What is one of the biggest life lessons you've learned so far that you could talk about for hours because you're so passionate about how learning it changed your life?

Day 18

Stop Playing Small and Let People Judge You

You're not here to be good. You're here to be real.
That is the real meaning of your life.
—Steve Siler

oday we're cracking open one of the biggest blocks that keeps powerful empaths invisible: The Bleeding Heart Block.

It's the cage of codependency, people-pleasing, and hypersensitivity that whispers: *Don't upset anyone. Don't rock the boat. Stay small and safe.*

It stems from terror—fear of hurting others, fear of rejection, fear of being misunderstood.

But here's the real tragedy:

In trying not to hurt anyone, you end up hurting yourself.

You dilute your message.

You lose your power.

You become invisible.

Many empaths who are sharing their message notice: *I'm posting, showing up … but it feels like no one sees me.*

This happens when you dilute your real message to keep others comfortable. You haven't yet had the courage to say what you *really* want to say.

The truth is simple: If you hold back your truth, people can feel it—and the result is crickets, not connection.

The solution isn't to people-please better. The solution is to *let people judge you.*

You must trust that your *intention* behind what you're sharing is enough.

If your heart is pure—if you're sharing from love, service, or healing—you are doing your job. How others receive it is not your responsibility.

When you try to control how people see you, you step into psychic trespassing: invading their space with worry, overthinking, and manipulation.

This leaks your power. And even worse, as I learned the hard way from a shaman in Peru, you energetically link up with their energy, which makes you susceptible to their limiting judgments and beliefs. What this means is if they are in fact judging or criticizing you, you end up absorbing that harmful energy like a sponge. One of the reasons I'm so passionate about this book and its message is to help you go from sponge to lighthouse. You're not here to be a sponge, soaking up an insecure world. You're here to shine from within, to be self-effulgent rather than self-critical.

Freedom comes when you trust yourself enough to let people have their reactions, their judgments, and their own experience.

You stop living their lives for them—and fully commit to living yours.

Let them judge you. It's not your business what stories they make up. It's not your responsibility to protect everyone from discomfort. It's not your job to be liked by everyone.

Your only job is to share what you know with a pure heart.

I know it's easier said than done, which is why in the next section of this book, I'll be giving you a powerful practice to overcome fear of being judged and embody calm regardless of outward circumstances.

For now, keep in mind …

Real leadership requires real courage. People can only connect with you when you're actually being *you*. But, what do you do when you feel afraid? When you just want to be liked? When reaching for the good-girl mask and peacekeeper identity comes on strong? How do you let people judge you when you fear being a bad person or unintentionally hurting someone?

If people's judgments make you second-guess yourself, remember this invaluable lesson:

One of my spiritual teachers, Sadhguru Shankaracharya, points to something that may be hard to hear at first, but liberating once you let it sink in: You can't control the outcome of what you do, say, or put into the world. The only thing you can control is your *purity of intention*. He says, "The intention behind your words and actions is often more significant than the words and actions themselves."

Before you post, teach, or share, check in to see that your intention is pure. Reflect:

- Do I want recognition? Consolation? Attention?
- Am I trying to build myself up or get something?
- Is what I'm sharing all about me instead of for them?

If your answers are *yes* to these questions and it's all about you, these are examples of skewed or egocentric intentions, of being a *follower of fear*.

Conversely, you can ask …

- What's my motivation for saying what I'm saying? Is it to help others?
- Is my intention pure?
- Am I speaking from love, generosity, or service?

If yes—then *go for it.* This is you being a *Leader of Love.*
And after that: LET PEOPLE JUDGE YOU.

If you're speaking from love, service, or healing—then you get
to trust that's enough. On the flip side, if you're seeking approval,
trying to pump yourself up, get something, or hurt someone, this
is not pure. Remember, every time you share is a choice between
being a *follower of fear* who is trying to get approval or a *Leader of
Love* who generously shares to empower or inspire others.

Your New Rule to Confidently
Be a Visible Empath

Before you post, speak, or show up anywhere, ask yourself one
question: *Is my intention pure?*

If it's yes—then go for it. Let the chips fall where they may.
Let people judge you. Let them get uncomfortable.

You're not here to babysit everyone's emotions. You are here
to lead.

Every time you let yourself be seen—even by people who misunderstand you—and accept yourself in the process, you reclaim another piece of your power. Every time you stop managing everyone else's perception, you step more fully into your destiny. Right now there are people who need to hear your story and message from you—not someone else. There's something about you that makes what you're sharing digestible for a particular group of people. Focus on serving the people who need and appreciate what you know.

Will some people judge you? Sure.

Will some people thank the heavens for you? Sure.

Let people have their own experience.

Let them judge you. Let them misunderstand you. Let them gossip. Let them love you. Let them get you. Let them reject you. Let them praise you. Let them be them, and you, beautiful lighthouse, be you!

It's none of your business what they feel about you. Their reactions are not proof of your worth. They're simply a reflection of where *they* are—not who *you* are. As spiritual teacher Leonard Jacobson powerfully taught me, their judgments are a statement about them, demonstrating that they're currently lost in the energy of judgment or criticism in that moment. That. Is. All.

For empaths especially, way too much weight is placed on others' perceptions. It's a surefire way to diminish yourself, because **nothing will make you feel smaller than letting others define you.** Defining yourself is your job!

Personal Story on How I Learned to Play Small

When I was a little girl, my life looked like a dream from the outside: Beautiful beach house. Loving father and sister. Lots of wonderful friends. Good grades. Perfect health. A closet filled with cute clothes and toys.

At the same time, my mother was homeless. And even at six years old, I carried guilt. *Why do I have so much when she has nothing?*

That guilt wrapped itself around my light. A belief took root: *It's wrong to shine too brightly. It's bad to have it good.*

Fast-forward a few years. At twelve, I went from a small private school on acres of lush land lined by the intracoastal where we went sailing in catamarans for P.E. class to a huge public school—3,000 students, gun fights in the halls, no windows in a cinder-block building.

And even though I stayed true to myself—sweet, spunky, pink-shirted—my very existence triggered people.

Within days, a tough girl glared across the room and threatened me: "You in the pink—flip your hair one more time and I'll kick your ass after school."

I hadn't said a word. I was simply *being me.* And right there, my nervous system got the message loud and clear: *Being seen is dangerous. Don't. Stand. Out!*

Playing Small Feels Safer ...
But Costs You Everything

After that, I learned to play it safe.

- Scan the room.
- Shrink my energy.
- Be very careful about what I say or do.
- Definitely don't touch that thick, wild mane of yours.
- Keep everyone comfortable.

I thought people-pleasing would protect me. But all it did was hurt me.

Every time you shrink to fit someone else's comfort, you rob the world of your brilliance. Every time you silence your authentic voice, you cut yourself—and others—off from the healing you came here to bring.

Your job is not to dim. Your job is to *shine anyway.*

If you have a calling to bring something beautiful, healing, or inspiring to our world, it's because you're intrinsically designed to be the good news. This requires a courageous quitting of the good-girl game. Good girls can't genuinely bring good news. The real good news is delivered through real people. Playing a good-girl persona is false. It's not you. It's holding you back. It held me back for years—decades! It's not only disingenuous, it also robs pained people of the medicine your message carries. You are the servant of your message. Take solace in this and gain confidence from it! Your message is within you for a reason. Sharing it isn't about you. It isn't about how many people like you or misunderstand you. It's not about being revered or validated. It's about recognizing that you have some unique lessons that your life prepared you to gain, master, and pay forward. You have something valuable to share, and this is your time to share it.

Playing the good girl or shrinking oneself is a trauma response. Can you breathe some compassion into your body, heart, and mind? It all served its function. And now, what if you genuinely let people have their opinions, while releasing the attempts to micromanage people's opinions of you, and instead sing your glorious message from the proverbial rooftop!

Today's Video Diary Prompt

If I gave zero sh* (beeps) about people liking or disliking me, the message I would sing from the rooftops is …

Love note: Let yourself explore here. Your conscious mind might not know the answer. If you give yourself a chance to speak spontaneously, you might discover something deeper that you didn't even know you're called to be a voice for.

Day 19

Healing the Persecution Wound

You never change things by fighting the existing reality.
To change something, build a new model
that makes the existing model obsolete.
—Buckminster Fuller

The fifth core visibility block, the Persecution Wound, sometimes referred to as the Witch Wound, is a collective spiritual trauma unconsciously affecting many deep souls. This terror sits squarely in the throat chakra, the energetic center of authentic self-expression. The origins reach far back into human history when people were silenced, punished, or even killed for having deep intuitive gifts, having a deeper connection with the wisdom of nature, or for sharing spiritual ideas and energy.

When the throat chakra is congested with fear, doubt, or ancestral memory, it can feel like you're bottling up truth after truth, idea after idea, unsure how to voice them—or if it's even safe to.

The solution to this block is to stay practiced in expressing yourself authentically in a safe space, without editing yourself or concerning yourself with how people are seeing you. What I mean by *stay practiced* is to have a daily habit or ritual of exploring and sharing your authentic voice without an agenda. For me personally, I chant, sing, or hum each morning. This isn't for anyone to hear. This is for me, the expansion of my energy, and my own freedom. I allow whatever wants to come through me to move.

As a speaker, as someone who is visible, your voice is your instrument, as is your body. Just like a pianist tunes the piano, you can tune your voice daily by speaking unedited, making sound without it needing to sound good, and expressing yourself without it having to be beneficial or pleasing to somebody. This is for you and your instrument!

Making video diaries, as we've been doing for over two weeks now, is a great way to stay practiced in authentic self-expression and clear your throat chakra channels. Way beyond this book, I suggest using the video diary practice any time you feel the need to clear blocked energy in your instrument (aka body), especially your throat. I make video diaries regularly. I love to *dump and delete*. Oftentimes, I'll make a video diary during my daily walks or from my car when I feel a dense or conflicted energy inside me. I speak the unspeakable in the parking lot of a market before walking in or while sitting under a tree in nature. Anywhere works as long as there's privacy so you can speak unedited. Then, when I delete it, I imagine whatever block was sitting in my throat chakra being cleared away once and for all. Poof!

Whether it's chanting, singing spontaneous lyrics, roaring, whispering, ululating, or talking freely into a voice memo or camera—*let the sound move through you*. Not to perform. Not to please. But to *liberate*.

Again, this practice isn't about being polished—it's about being *real*. Your voice is your instrument. *Tune your voice* daily by letting it express without the filter of performance or approval.

Make video diaries.

Use voice notes.

Sing off-key.

Speak the unspeakable.

Say the things that have been stuck in your throat for years.

Let it be messy.

Let it be raw.

Because **underneath the clutter is *your message***. And that message is your medicine—not just for others, but for *you*.

Visibility becomes your healing path when you celebrate your expression no matter what the response. That's how you become unshakable. Just like diamonds are born under pressure and butterflies hatch in friction, freedom is found *inside* the act of being seen as your whole self.

To heal the Persecution Wound, you're invited to become your own refuge—a place of unwavering safety you return to whenever the fear of others' judgment threatens to silence you. Instead of being hypervigilant about how you're seen or perceived, learn to turn your awareness inward. Become vigilant about what your own mind is doing. When you notice it slipping into self-criticism, overthinking, or fear, gently hold yourself in a space of safety and compassion. This is where real healing begins: not in fearing the outside world, but in mothering yourself rather than limiting yourself.

Rewriting Your Vocal Blueprint

Each time you express yourself without editing, you reclaim your energy. You rewrite your energetic blueprint. You clear the debris clogging your voice, your clarity, and your confidence. I remember I used to stand tall in the center of my living room, imagining a sold-out venue, speaking words of inspiration without a script. I loved discovering the message as it came through, the version of myself who was not trying to please others, and the raw, honest power of my voice. It was so much easier to access my valuable voice when no one was watching. Every time I did this, I felt myself grow as a speaker.

Try this:

- Pretend you're on stage, speaking to thousands.
- Let your most bold, truthful, uncensored voice rise up.
- Express yourself without the edit button—feel the freedom in your body when you stop holding back.

Whether you hum, whisper, roar, or proclaim—do it for *you*. This is more than vocal practice. It's *spiritual strength training*. It's confidence building through embodiment.

When you do this consistently, you stop needing approval. You stop fearing the moment someone doesn't like what you said. Because you've already become *your own safety*.

The Practice: Connect Throat and Womb Energy

There was a period in my life when I was grinding my teeth so hard at night that I'd wake up unable to open my mouth. I had to pry my jaw open with my hands just to remove my nightguard. This was during a time of exponential business growth. On the outside, everything looked successful, but inside, I was carrying immense pressure to perform. I was glued to screens instead of getting sunshine, endlessly sitting instead of swimming, and though I longed to be outdoors, I was tethered to my computer. I had become disconnected from my body, my sensuality, my pleasure.

In hindsight, all of that jaw tension was a clear somatic signal. Energetically, it reflected the relationship between the throat chakra—our center of expression—and the second chakra, the seat of our pleasure and creativity. My locked jaw served as a somatic signal that I needed to cultivate safety within myself by prioritizing pleasure and self-care over external demands and pressure.

Anatomically, the throat and pelvis are connected through the fascial network, deep core muscles, and the vagus nerve—key players in both our voice and our sense of safety. Tension held in the pelvic floor or womb (second chakra) often manifests as tightness in the jaw and throat muscles (throat chakra), restricting authentic expression. This mind-body link means that releasing stored emotions or physical tightness in the pelvis can unlock freer vocal expression, while opening the throat can help ground and stabilize the body. Understanding and working with this connection supports a more integrated, embodied way of speaking your truth with confidence and ease.

Take a moment now:

- Place one hand just below your navel.
- Place the other hand at your throat.
- Inhale deeply. Feel breath move past the throat and into the womb space.
- Hold. Receive. Exhale with a sound.

Feel the energetic mirror between these two power centers. Let them harmonize. The more grounded your creative energy is, the more authentic power can rise and move through your voice. The more comfortable you are with your sensuality, the smoother your voice will be.

Let your voice be the channel your soul has always wanted to speak through.

Visibility Isn't Performance —It's Liberation

The win isn't the standing ovation. The win is applauding yourself.

The win isn't working diligently under pressure. The win is being in your pleasure.

The win isn't how people respond. The win is *that you did it.*

That you said the thing. That you showed up. That you didn't edit or overprepare. That you *chose* to free your voice.

The world needs your message, but more importantly—*you need your message.*

You deserve to know what it feels like to be fully expressed.

So roar like a lion. Whisper like a priestess. Speak like the universe is listening.

Because it is.

And now—so are you. To your own heart and soul.

So now when you speak in front of others, you won't need them to see or get you. You've got that covered. You see and get yourself. It's a daily practice. Now, you can focus on serving the message and those who need it.

Today's Video Diary Prompt ☑️

What would the boldest version of you say—and to whom?

Day 20

How to Free Yourself from the Comparison Cage

*I slept and dreamt that life was joy. I awoke and saw that life
was service. I acted and behold, service was joy.*
—Rabindranath Tagore

oday, it's time to free yourself from the sixth visibility
block—the Comparison Cage—by realizing you are
beyond comparison!

Take a deep breath.

Say it with me now …

I am beyond comparison!

The more *you* that you are, the more impactful your message is and the more your body and spirit thrive. Integrity, which is the alignment of your thoughts, actions, and words, is healing for your entire being. Conversely, going against yourself can be destructive. For a long time, I tried to mimic my business coach because of how impressive, financially empowered, and impactful she was. Learning from her made me exponentially more money, but trying to do it her way like an Energizer Bunny that never sleeps sent me into a downward health spiral. My authentic nature is way more feminine, and what I've come to discover is that my audience loves that about me. It's actually part of what draws those I can help to me because they see themselves in me, or they want more feminine energy to balance their overdrive.

I faced this block early on as well, when I first started making videos. I tried to emulate other creators I respected, like speaker, author, and entrepreneur Marie Forleo. I'd put on a show with my videos, which made speaking and teaching feel more like an acting job. It felt safe to hide behind a persona, and the bright side was that I had fun with it. Since I came from an acting background, performing felt more comfortable than being myself. The downside is that I didn't think I was enough in comparison to leaders I respected. I thought I needed to add something to myself in order to be successful or worthy of engagement.

I'd muster up a larger energy as I imagined talking to a grand audience like hers. Of course it's important to bring enthusiasm to our work. However, there's a fine line between feeling genuinely excited to share the value you're about to provide and putting on a show because you don't think who you are is enough in comparison to others. I eventually discovered that I was caught in a trauma response, believing I had to perform or match up to someone else's standard to be successful. This pattern started as a highly sensitive toddler being pulled into commercial auditions and onto stages where I was forced to pretend. The performance was a block—an exhausting one, no less—because it wasn't allowing me to enjoy putting my attention on something generative—enjoying my life and serving my message!

Like you, I'm a full-on original. It took me many years to realize that the people I'm here to help want the real me. In the same way, your ideal clients, audience, and students want the real you. This is your moment to step out of the Comparison Cage, throw your arms up in celebration, and shine as the real you!

Repeat after me:

I am beyond comparison.

I am a full-on original.

There is only one of me.

This is my time to set myself free and be all that I truly am!

Say it again until it lands. Because the truth is—there's only one *you* for a reason. You don't have to prove yourself. You just have to *be* yourself. The people who are here to learn from or be inspired by you need you to be exactly as you are. Your exact weight, height, accent, skin color, educational background or lack thereof … every detail that makes up who you presently are is what makes you relatable and magnetic to your right people.

Focus on who you're here to serve and the message that could wholeheartedly serve that *one person* or ideal client you're here to help. The *me* takes care of itself when you focus on serving your authentic, value-based message. The sacred truth that you're unlike anyone else will emerge as you focus on setting your Soul Signature Story free, which also holds the teachings and wisdom you're uniquely here to share. In one of my most loved programs, Confident Course Creation School™, I watch student after student shift into confidence as they birth their unique body of work and Soul Signature Story. Birthing your unique body of work, mining up the stories that you've lived through, and clarifying the empowering lessons is transformative, clearing away the pain of comparison. The ego loves to use comparison as a way to keep us safe and small.

And, here's the thing …

Once you know the value of your voice by clarifying your unique message, the ego's fear loses its grip.

Once you see what you're made of, you can't unsee it.

Once you own that you're one of a kind and beyond comparison, there's no going back.

This is your opportunity to go beyond the Comparison Cage by owning your specialized knowledge and uniqueness. We'll be going into your unique story in the final phase of this book. If you want to explore more deeply, you can get my free *Using Your Story to Help Others Workshop* at https://www.thediamondprocess.com/story

Find Your Valuable Voice by Speaking to One Person

Focusing on speaking to or sharing your message with *one* person can give you instant clarity and confidence. If you focus on a crowd, it may bring up excess fear, weigh you down with pressure, and create performative anxiety. When you focus on sharing your message with one specific person who needs it instead, you'll find it so much easier to be yourself rather than putting on a show. It also makes your message magnetic. There's a popular marketing phrase that says, "When you talk to everyone, you reach no one." This is because when your message is too vague or broad, you lose the ability to connect with any one human being. When you speak specifically to one person, the relatability of your message will make it spread like wildfire, touching the people who also struggle with the problem you're helping them solve.

Whenever I do a livestream, teach a class, or get on stage, even if I'm broadcasting to thousands, I don't think about masses of people. Holy heavens—that would buckle my knees and collapse me into insecure thinking. Instead, I focus on one beloved student—someone I care about deeply who is getting great results from working together or someone I see potential in—and I speak to her. When you serve from this place of love, service, and presence, comparison loses its grip.

The reason so many stay silent isn't because they lack value—it's because they don't know where to begin. So, instead of creating, they get stuck in consuming other people's content, which reinforces the Comparison Cage. Watching from the sidelines is painful when deep down you know you're meant to take center stage to shine the light on a valuable message. Your soul speaking is akin to a roaring fire, warming those who gather around it. That fire that burns within you is meant to light up the world, but when silenced, it can fester, burning us up inside.

Want to know where to start with voicing your message? Let's break it down into five steps.

Five Steps to Getting Clarity on Your Message That Moves Others

1) Release the idea that you're talking to an audience and select *one* person you can truly serve and are inspired to speak to.

2) Put yourself in their shoes and discover what their biggest struggle is and what they truly want. Even better, ask them what they struggle with and what they want.

3) Make content that helps them solve their problem or create their vision using storytelling, teachings, and actionable tools.

4) Turn on your camera and imagine that you're speaking directly to one person you can help and who you enjoy helping.

5) Share the content from your heart and celebrate your one-of-a-kind self!

This is your moment to stand tall. To be the lighthouse. To let your unique message shine.

When you focus on *who* you can help and wholeheartedly share your valuable voice with them, comparison fades away and the people who need you most can finally find you.

Today's Video Diary Prompt ☑

The person I'm most inspired to help and share my message with is _____ because …

Let that person be your guiding star. The one you're showing up for and serving your message to.

How to Instantly Overcome Perfectionism

Forget your perfect offering.
There's a crack, a crack in everything.
That's how the light gets in.
—Leonard Cohen

I write this chapter tenderly because I thought I had already broken through the Perfectionist Headlock.

After all, here I am writing an entire book about healing and visibility, and I believed I had cleared enough of the blocks to consider myself free. But healing is a spiral, not a straight line—and the Perfectionist Headlock, the block I've struggled with the most, came back for me when I least expected it.

I recently took part in a sound healing certification program when our teacher announced that we'd all be going to karaoke one night—not just for fun, but as an exercise in freeing our voices. I froze. I had never done karaoke before, and the last time I sang an entire song on a stage I was 13, singing and dancing— things I used to *love* before life's challenges tamed me.

I tried everything to avoid going up. When I saw my name inching up the karaoke queue, I started planning my escape. It was late, there were still people ahead of me, and I had a million excuses ready. But then the teacher said something that cracked me open: "This isn't about how you sound, Veronica. This is about courage. Do it for courage, not for perfection."

That, I could work with. I couldn't control perfection. But I could choose courage.

Still, I was terrified. I watched another woman in our group step up, trembling. Her voice barely came out, but her energy was radiant. She was shaking, but she stayed. She lifted her arms and invited us to sing with her. That moment made her my hero. I could see her success had nothing to do with perfection. It was her courage, her joy! My childhood programming around needing to be perfect to be lovable started melting off of my shoulders. I hugged her afterward, celebrating her courage— and then she turned to me and said, "Okay, now it's your turn."

I admitted I was scared and about to leave. But instead of letting me go, she pulled me outside away from the crowded bar and said, "Let's practice." As we faced a chill in the mountain air, she wrapped one of her arms around me as she played my song on her phone and held space for me as I sang, shaky and raw.

She told me I had a beautiful voice. Yet, she could also see how scared I was. I had one minute left before it was my turn to sing. I sensed her scrambling to help, "Remember to breathe," she hollered as I ran into the bar. I breathed as I slowed to a strut, playing it cool as the DJ called my name. Steps away from the stage, she caught up to me with four final words that felt like a lifeline: "Call on your angels."

I don't usually rely on something I can't see or control, but I knew my own willpower wasn't going to help me here. Right before going up, I whispered, "If I have a flock of angels, or even one guardian angel, please help me. Help me set my voice free. Help me have fun on that stage."

And then I did it.

I got on stage. I confessed it was my first time. I took a deep breath, closed my eyes, lifted my chin, and started to sing. The song was *Hero* by Mariah Carey—a song I used to sing to myself over 15 years ago when I was going through a hard time. As I sang, I kept my eyes on the lyrics, one hand in my pocket, the other gripping the mic so my shaking didn't show. My body was in fear, but my heart was in courage.

Halfway through, I looked up and saw the entire bar— silent. Everyone had their phones out with their flashlights on, waving them like little candles. It was surreal. I hadn't felt that connected to my voice—or to that younger, brazen 12-year-old me—in decades. It was electric. I got off stage shaking. People cheered, hugged me, and said things like, "You're a star," and "You were born to do this."

But I couldn't believe them.

My brain told me they were pitying me, that they were just being kind. That I was embarrassing, and they were in on a joke I didn't understand. Even when one of the facilitators— someone very grounded and honest—told me I had real talent and should pursue a vocal coach, it barely cracked the wall. He said, "I go to karaoke bars all the time. This doesn't happen. The whole bar turned for you. That doesn't just happen."

That night, I went home and rewatched the recording someone took of me—over and over again. I couldn't tell if it was good or delusional. I sent it to someone I trust deeply, and the next morning he replied: "A star is reborn." And again, I didn't believe it. I thought he was being kind, funny, or trying to soften the blow of what I still believed was a train wreck.

The vulnerability hangover hit hard. Shame crept in. I felt drained, exposed, and humiliated that I had even sent the video. I retracted it. I considered skipping class entirely the next day, but I didn't. I showed up—30 minutes late, head low, heart racing.

And when I walked into the room?

The whole class was *waiting* for me. Playing the song *Hero*. As I entered, the entire group looked at me and said, "You're a hero." I couldn't believe it. I literally ducked down, trying to hide behind a table. But they kept cheering. I peeked up, and these powerful, soulful people were celebrating me with genuine joy.

I finally let it in.

In front of everyone, I shared everything—the shame, the fear, the voice in my head that told me I wasn't enough unless I was perfect. I told them how perfectionism had ruled me my whole life. And how I had internalized a dangerous belief as a child: that imperfection meant rejection. That flaw meant failure. That not being perfect could get you cast out and left behind—just as I saw happen to my mother.

But that night, something shifted.

I laid the perfectionist to rest. I let her go.

And in her place, I chose courage.

A week after that imperfect-but-electric karaoke moment, I shared the story with my longtime mentor—someone who used to direct me in plays. I told him how confused I was that the audience lit up their phones and connected so deeply, even though my singing was far from perfect. He looked at me and said, "You still don't get it, do you? It's your essence. You bared your soul up there. You weren't performing—you were being real. That's what moved them." His words cracked something open in me. For so long, I believed my value on stage—or in any spotlight—came from being polished and perfect. But that night taught me (and may be teaching you now) that people aren't looking for a perfect performance. They're longing to feel something real. And when you dare to be fully seen, soul-first, your voice, your song, your message moves people.

This chapter isn't just a story for you, the reader—I'm moving through it alongside you. This journey we're on isn't about being perfect. Not even about being perfect at *clearing visibility blocks*. This is about choosing courage. It's about choosing life—messy, beautiful, fully expressed life. It's about pleasure, fun, expansion, vulnerability, and being kind to yourself as you grow.

However true what I'm sharing with you is, in practical terms, what do you do when you're caught in the Perfectionist Headlock and the fear feels so real that it stops you?

What's the solution to the Perfectionist Headlock?

The solution to the Perfectionist Headlock is to give the perfectionist a well-deserved vacation.

That's right—send her off to Barbados with a piña colada and a good novel. In my programs, I often say: "For these six weeks, let the perfectionist rest."

And then? "Go make a glorious mess. We're playing in the sandbox!"

Fail. Flop. Fumble forward. Do a wildly mediocre job and celebrate it—just like me on that karaoke stage—not because you don't care, but because you're doing the very thing 99% of people are too afraid to do: show up imperfectly and take action anyway. Courage!

Your imperfections are not liabilities. They are the bridges to connection, trust, and resonance.

Recently, one woman in my membership made a video from her living room. Behind her? A mountain of unfolded laundry, kids' toys, and goddess knows what else. She smiled and said, "I was about to clean up before hitting record, but then I thought—No. This is me right now. I'm done waiting to be perfect."

It was real. It was raw. I loved her even more after that.

Let me tell you something true:

It may feel safe to your ego, but it's deeply unsafe to others. People don't want a polished mask. They want someone real. Someone human. Someone who shows them that it's okay to play full-out and still be in process. This is probably why the whole karaoke bar turned on their flashlights and people were so present with me. It's not because my voice was perfect. It's because I sang with soul. I sang with courage. I sang with my whole heart. I went for it!

The authenticity created relatability.

The imperfection created connection.

Hiding behind perfection is a disservice to yourself, your message, and those you're here to serve.

It drains your confidence.

It disconnects you from your creativity.

And it keeps you small—afraid to start, afraid to share, afraid to be seen.

The way through this visibility block—*which is directly tied to the crown chakra and your connection to your higher self*—is to *redefine success.*

Instead of basing your success on whether or not you did something perfectly, hit all the metrics, or got exceptional results, let your success be the only thing you can control:

doing the thing you're called to do, but are afraid to do, and celebrating yourself in the process.

I've seen so many brilliant empaths, coaches, creatives, and healers stay stuck for years because they weren't willing to start small or risk a meager beginning. They had meaningful messages to share, but the ideal version in their minds felt so far off, they couldn't begin.

I get it. Writing this book brought up the perfectionist in me.

I had a call with my publishing coach a few weeks before a major deadline. She asked me to share my screen and show her my draft. I felt nervous. Embarrassed. The manuscript was far from polished. I hadn't written daily as I promised myself I would. My inner critic screamed, *Real writers write every day. You're not a real writer.*

But when I shared that with her, she looked at me and said, *You need to lower your expectations.*

What? I expected her to push me harder. Instead, she offered grace. She suggested I aim for three or four writing sessions a week, not seven. Suddenly, the pressure lifted. I felt seen. Encouraged. Reinspired.

Funny, isn't it? She coached me the same way I coach my clients—but I hadn't offered myself that same compassion.

That day, even after writing already, I wrote for two extra hours. Not out of guilt. But out of joy. Because success breeds success—*when it's defined in a way that serves you.*

Redefining success is a powerful way to escape the Perfectionist Headlock. Expect mistakes. Let them become markers of growth rather than signs of shame.

When you stop measuring success by things you can't control—how many people comment, how much money you make, or whether others approve—you create freedom.

Instead, define success based on what *you* can control: your courage, your consistency, your commitment to sharing something of value ... and most importantly, how kind you are to yourself in the process. This not only frees you to do what you came here to do, it also allows those who need what you have to be given the chance to receive it!

When my clients redefine success this way, everything changes. They stop hiding. They stop overthinking. They start sharing with joy and showing up with boldness.

It's like flipping on a light switch. The lighthouse goes on! It might look like magic, but it's really just alignment.

Your success doesn't depend on likes, followers, or feedback. Those are the *icing*.

You—your freedom, your full expression, your commitment to showing up with love and truth—*are the cake*.

And that energetic shift? It's magnetic.

When you're fully engaged in what you're doing—not waiting to be perfect, but proud of being *in motion*—that's when people lean in. That's when your message begins to ripple. That's when strangers in a bar turn on their flashlight and sway along to the song you're singing, even when you can't hit the notes. That's when you become truly unforgettable.

Today's Video Diary Prompt ☑

Who do you love watching, listening to, or learning from who has flaws and doesn't hide them? What is it specifically that makes them so compelling to you?

Phase IV

BEING THE GOOD NEWS

The Bedrock of All Visibility Blocks

To love oneself is the beginning of a lifelong romance.
—Oscar Wilde

ven though we've explored the seven core visibility blocks and the practical solutions for each, there's really only *one root cause* beneath them all—the bedrock upon which all visibility fears find ground. At the bottom of it all, there is one single, fear-based belief that holds you back from fully expressing the message you came here to share with the world.

Every visibility block stems from one source: the fear of rejection.

But not in the way you might think.

For years, I taught that the secret to confident visibility was overcoming the fear of being rejected by others. And at the surface level, that makes sense. After all, the idea of putting yourself out there—only to be met with criticism, indifference, or judgment—is enough to pipe down even the most practiced voice.

But something wasn't quite adding up. After working with hundreds of coaches, healers, empaths, and conscious creatives—people who had meaningful messages yet remained invisible—I began to notice a deeper pattern.

It wasn't the *external* rejection they feared most.

It was the *internal rejection* that happened *afterward*.

What I came to understand is that **the bedrock of all visibility resistance isn't a fear of other people rejecting you. It's the fear of rejecting yourself when you *feel* judged.** It's the fear that *you* will abandon, criticize, or emotionally punish yourself in response to how others respond—or don't respond—to your voice.

The Hidden Wound: When We Persecute Ourselves

The Persecution Wound we talked about in chapters 12 and 19 emphasizes the fear of judgment or harm from others. At the root of all visibility blocks, however, is the fear of *self-persecution*—the attempt to avoid beating yourself up when others reject you.

This self-persecution can be subtle. It shows up as second-guessing. As staying quiet in rooms where you have wisdom. As performing for approval instead of showing up as you truly are. Other times, it's not so subtle. It shows up as thrashing yourself, doubting yourself, or ruminating after giving a livestream or speaking up in a meeting.

When we say we fear public speaking, what we're really saying is *I'm afraid of others judging me harshly and believing them.* This is the self-persecution we spend our lives trying to avoid. Not the trolls in the comments. Not the silence after a heartfelt post. Not the unsubscribes or the unsubtle eye rolls. No, the part that truly stings—the part we *fear*—is what we do to ourselves afterward.

The overanalyzing. The spiral of self-criticism. The emotional crash after the livestream. The thoughts like, *Why did I say it like that?* or *I should've done more,* or worse, *No one cares.*

If you're like most sensitive, purpose-driven people, you've learned to avoid these spirals by staying in your comfort zone. You rationalize, you wait for the "perfect" time, or you throw out tiny versions of your truth, hoping no one notices. But what's really happening is this: You've outsourced your safety. You've given your inner anchor away.

Early in my coaching career, I taught one of my very first online courses. One of the students was also a friend, and after class she invited me to lunch. Over the meal she asked if she could give me some feedback—and then spent the next half hour listing everything I had done "wrong."

I had poured myself into those classes. I spent days creating beautiful slides, over-delivering content, and answering every student's questions. So when she told me it was "too much," I felt crushed. My mind spiraled with self-criticism: *I gave too much and it still wasn't enough. I'm failing. I should quit.*

That spiral wasn't new. It was the same pattern I had lived through as an actress—reliving every misstep, criticizing myself relentlessly, and tearing down my own confidence. However valuable and well-meaning, her words stung, but the real wound came from what I did to myself afterward.

At that point, I didn't have the emotional balancing tool I'll be teaching you in the next chapter. It took painful moments like that one for me to realize that unless I learned to regulate my nervous system and be kind to myself, I would burn out completely. Eventually, I devoted myself to becoming my own safety and putting my frequency first, and everything shifted. I stopped leaving visibility experiences drained and defeated, and instead began to feel energized by them.

That experience taught me something crucial: Rejection doesn't destroy us—the way we treat ourselves afterward does.

When we fear our own emotional responses, we dim our light to avoid the aftershock. We get overly busy so there's no time to vulnerably go for what we want. If we do make the time, we try to control perceptions. We censor our message. We overperfect. And in doing so, we unconsciously disconnect from our power.

But here's the truth:

To be fully visible, to own your voice, and to become unapologetically magnetic, you get to become your own source of safety and also have a *why* that is bigger than your fear. This is what I call your *Evolutionary Why*, which we went deep into on day 7. Your Evolutionary Why is the deeper soul-call behind your visibility—not to grow your following or hit a certain income goal, but to grow *you*. As an empath, healer, or coach, your nervous system craves safety and authenticity, not performance. That's why **the most powerful reason to share your voice isn't to prove yourself—it's to *free* yourself.**

When your why is to become your own safety, to regulate your energy in real time, and to show up for yourself with compassion, you create a sacred space where healing happens through the act of visibility itself. The path of visibility accelerates your personal and spiritual growth because it invites every hidden part of you into the light—and challenges you to meet it with presence and compassion. But if you stay in hiding, fearing failure or judgment, this opportunity to grow through action never arrives. You can't fail at this—because every time you share your valuable voice and celebrate yourself in the process, you expand. You evolve. And that is a win which no algorithm or audience size can ever measure.

When you become your own source of safety in the spotlight, you're not just sharing your message that moves others—you're becoming more embodied, more awake, and more *you*.

Ask yourself: Can it be enough—right now—to simply breathe deeply, stay present through discomfort, and gently regulate your nervous system as you take bold, imperfect action?

If your answer is yes—even just a whisper of yes—you're already ahead of the game. You're choosing a different path. One that doesn't chase distant milestones but savors the *now*. And ironically, this is the very path that leads to real, sustainable results—in your life, your creativity, and your business.

To actually enjoy the journey, step by step?

Yes. What a radical idea in a world obsessed with the finish line.

No one else can give you the stability and safety you seek. No number of likes, shares, or testimonials will ever substitute for the steadiness you offer yourself.

This is where *emotional regulation* becomes your greatest ally.

It's not about shutting down your emotions—it's about learning to hold space for them with grace. To stay connected to yourself *even when you feel exposed*. To be the unwavering presence within your own nervous system, no matter what's happening around you.

This is the key that unlocks true confidence, embodied leadership, and lasting visibility. And the good news is, it's not as complicated as you might think.

Everything shared in this chapter is preparation for a simple, powerful nervous system regulation tool I'm giving you in the next chapter that's helped countless clients shift years of visibility struggle in just a few days. It's gentle, effective, and rooted in compassion—and it might just be the missing link you've been looking for.

But for now, I want you to remember one thing:

You are the masterpiece—not the rubble.

You are not the version of yourself who shrinks in fear. You are the one who is rising from the cracks of it.

Today's Video Diary Prompt

Imagine talking to someone who doubts themselves and whom you see as having potential or talent. Think of someone specific whom you love, who wants to share their voice on video but is afraid. Why should they share their voice? Why does their voice matter? Look straight into the lens of your camera, take a breath, and speak directly to them from your heart, sharing why it's important that they share their voice and are visible.

Take a breath and start with: *You know that secret desire in your heart to share your voice with others? Here's why I think you should go for it ...*

Once you're done, watch the video and receive the message for yourself.

How to Regulate Your Nervous System Using the 5 A's

Feelings come and go like clouds in a windy sky.
Conscious breathing is my anchor.
—Thich Nhat Hanh

In the previous chapter, we unveiled the truth, illuminating the real reason empaths don't feel safe being seen: The deepest root of visibility fear isn't rejection from others—it's *self-rejection*. That inner criticism that surfaces after you've shared your voice, the emotional spiral after a post or livestream, the subtle (or not-so-subtle) ways you abandon yourself when you feel exposed or judged.

This self-rejection is what truly keeps you from being visible—not the audience, the algorithm, or the offer. And unless you know how to hold yourself lovingly in emotionally activated moments, no amount of marketing strategy, under-eye concealer, or mindset hacks will bring lasting confidence.

So what do you do with that awareness? You learn to *become* the safety you've been seeking. You master emotional regulation.

The Power of Emotional Regulation

Imagine the life you could create once you're no longer afraid of how you feel.

When you know how to hold yourself through discomfort, your world expands. You access pleasure more deeply. You speak more freely. You create with more aliveness and courage.

To cultivate this kind of inner safety, it's important to first understand the two internal dimensions we all move between:

- **The Storyline**: Also called the timeline, this is your personal history—your childhood, past experiences, projections into the future. This mental realm is where most people live much of the time. This is where your inner critic lives, woven from old wounds and inherited beliefs like *I'm not enough,* or *I'll be rejected.*
- **The Lifeline**: This is the present moment—where your *Diamond Self,* or True Self, lives. It's loving, wise, and connected to Source. Attuning to the present moment, the Lifeline, anchors you in truth and confidence. From here, you're the lighthouse, not the sponge. Your physical body lives in the present moment, on the Lifeline, which is why grounding in your body is such a powerful way to embody true power.

If you're stuck in the Storyline, you're likely reliving the past on repeat, especially when visibility fears trigger you. Your nervous system can't tell the difference between emotional memory and present reality, so you default to old coping patterns like hiding, fawning, or criticizing yourself, which feeds self-rejection.

One of my clients—a gifted coach—committed to doing weekly livestreams for a full year. Brave, right? But every time she went live, she felt disappointed afterward. The audience engagement was low. People clicked out early. And without fail, she spiraled into self-doubt and harsh inner judgment. She'd come to nearly every session asking for a better strategy. Here's the thing: Her audience growth strategy wasn't the problem, her energy was.

What was happening?

She was unconsciously stuck on her Storyline—the inner child trying to win her perfectionist mother's approval.

Through our work, she learned to *emotionally regulate*. Instead of abandoning herself and chasing her next goal, she learned to *mother* her emotions and show up with soul. That shift changed everything: her energy, her magnetism, her relationships. She stopped performing and started *connecting*. Her energy changed. Her audience grew. Instead of chasing an income goal, she naturally stepped into it with frequency, not force.

I often say, "Your frequency is your #1 job." Being a coach, healer, mother, or leader of any kind is your second job. The energy you bring to what you do is primary! You can be doing all the *right* things externally, but if you're still judging yourself internally—trying to fix, edit, or silence your feelings—your confidence and magnetism will dim.

The 5 A's for Regulating Your Emotions

In this chapter, I'm excited to share a practice with you that I've taught to hundreds of clients and students—it's simple, repeatable, and it works to help you instantly reset to calm and confidence! This is a practical way to shift from emotional spirals into a state of embodied safety. Think of it like brushing your teeth. It's not something you do once, but something easy you do daily, or ideally morning and night. It's how you pivot from the Storyline to your Lifeline. You can use it when you wake up while still in bed, before a livestream, after receiving feedback, before falling asleep, or any time you feel off-center. This is a transformative practice you can slip in your backpack to use anytime you get stuck in fear, doubt, or a dysregulated nervous system.

Love note: If you are dealing with trauma, please work with a trauma-informed therapist. This practice is not a substitute for professional therapy.

Want me to directly guide you through this practice in an audio?

Download this gift of a guided "5A's for Regulating Your Nervous System and Embodying Confidence" here (thediamondprocess.com/regulate). Slip this audio gift into your back pocket, and try it for 5 days in a row to start (5 A's in Five Days). Practice it before or after you're visible, and watch how everything shifts—your energy, your magnetism, and your ability to receive what you deeply desire—all from a place of grounded safety.

The 5 A's to Regulating Your Emotions

1. Awareness

Place one hand on your heart, one on your belly. Research shows that physical touch lowers cortisol levels (the stress hormone) in the body. Your own physical touch can be just as effective as a hug from somebody you love.

Breathe as you hold yourself.

- Gently ask: ***What am I feeling right now?*** (Name the feeling.)

If you find it difficult to identify exactly what you're feeling, simply select one of the four primary feelings: anger, fear, joy, or sadness.

- ***Where do I feel it in my body?*** (Locate the feeling.)

If you feel the feeling in more than one place, I encourage you to focus on the location in your body that feels the most active.

Then place your hand over that spot, feel into it as you breathe, and whisper to yourself, *I'm here with you. I'm not leaving.*

This simple act of presence brings you to the *lifeline* and begins the process of healing and integrating a facet of yourself that's been orphaned, judged, or rejected. This is how you activate being the lighthouse—by being the light for you!

2. Authenticity

Let the emotion speak. Let there be space between you and the feeling. You are not the feeling. You are the mother, lover, or holder of it. You are the one witnessing it.

Start with: ***I feel (<u>emotion you named in step 1</u>) because***

_____.

You can do this internally, out loud, or through a video diary (for your eyes only). What is this part of you trying to say? Give the feeling a voice.

Think of the emotion as a child who just wants to be heard. Again, you are not the feeling. You are the one neutrally listening and holding it into safety.

You don't need to fix it—that causes more problems. This is an opportunity to see it with the same neutrality that you witness a cloud in the sky. Simply witness it with loving care and presence.

3. Allowance

Ask: ***Am I willing to allow this feeling to exist?***

You don't have to like it. Just allow it.

Emotions are like weather. You are the sky. Imagine trying to force the clouds out of the sky. Would that make any difference? No! The sky would never try to do that. The vast sky allows everything to exist without getting identified with it. The same thing goes with a healthy mother and her child. She allows her child to feel what the little one feels without making it about her or judging the matter. Her job is to be present, patient, and a safe place for her child to express themselves rather than trying to push the problem away. Allow. Witness. Release judgment. Breathe.

This is also what a lighthouse does. It doesn't leave the shore to rescue a boat in troubled waters. By being a still, grounded, illuminated force, it serves as a guiding light for the ships to find their way to safety.

4. Acceptance

Every feeling has an unmet need underneath it. Ask the feeling as if speaking to a vulnerable child: ***What do you need, sweetheart?***

Maybe it's rest. Maybe it's reassurance. Maybe it's silence, to be held, or space.

Listen. Stay curious. Discover.

When you meet your unmet needs—you begin to trust yourself. That's where true confidence is born. When you stop outsourcing acceptance by wishing your audience, family, or colleagues would praise you, and become a radical embrace for your multifaceted self, you become a rare force of love. This is especially true when you validate the place within you that you've been judging, shaming, or avoiding.

5. Appreciation

Finally, ask: ***What is the gift in this feeling?***

Sadness may have asked you to slow down. Anger may be pointing to a boundary that has been crossed. Fear may be revealing a limiting belief that has subconsciously been holding you back that it's time to clean up.

When you appreciate the message inside the mess, triggers become treasures. They become lifelines to more life force or messengers of wisdom that help you evolve, grow in confidence, and embody wholeness so you can confidently live your purpose and enjoy your life.

Over time, it will change how you show up in your business, in your relationships, and in your own skin.

You Are Not Your Storyline

When you offer yourself gentleness instead of judgment, you don't just regulate an emotion. You *rewrite your identity.*

You remind yourself:
I am not my emotions.
I am not my thoughts.
I am not my old story.
I am the loving presence.
The lighthouse.
I am valuable beyond measure.

And the more you become your own safety, the more your light shines without fear.

Today's Video Diary Prompt

What does Love want to say to the tender place inside you that fears rejection?

Close your eyes. Take a few grounding breaths. Then let your heart speak directly to that tender place—not to fix it, but to love it. Let love have the mic. No filters, no performance. Just genuine care.

Day 24

Ten Steps to Mapping Your Unique Transformational Story

*There is no greater agony than bearing
an untold story inside you.*
—Maya Angelou

Today we're exploring how to use your transformational story to help others. Many of the empaths, coaches, healers, artists, and spiritual teachers I work with struggle with confidence and clarity. They don't always know how to focus their energy or share their wisdom with impact. The beautiful truth is this: Clarity comes from within. Your *transformational story* is your map—and owning it unlocks your confidence.

Let's take a deep breath together.

Inhale.

Exhale.

My vision for you today is that what you learn moves you into joyfully sharing your gifts.

Once you understand and apply the structure of a transformational story, visibility becomes purposeful and empowering. It becomes *fun*.

You Already Have What You Need to Confidently Inspire Others

Have you ever made it through something difficult and discovered a powerful insight, new strength, or gift within yourself?

If yes, then you already have expertise. It's buried like treasure inside the challenges you've overcome.

Your lived experience is not just a personal triumph—it's a source of *credibility*. When you share your story in an intentional way that imparts wisdom, it resonates. It invites connection. It inspires action.

Many people rush to offer guidance or tools without first anchoring in their deeper *why*—the personal reason that fuels their message. Some call this *the why that makes you cry*. It's the deeper calling that compels you to share your story, not for attention, but to support those who are struggling with what you once faced yourself. When your message is rooted in lived experience and genuine empathy, it radiates authenticity and purpose. That's when what you say becomes magnetic.

My deeper *why* for writing this book is a vision I have of the world where empaths stop absorbing the pain around them and start radiating the light within them. We weren't built to be sponges—we were born to be lighthouses. When we remember this, we not only heal ourselves, we inspire the next generation to believe in the beauty of being fully alive—and how that alone could help them choose to stay, to grow, to thrive.

One of the problems so many empaths and bighearted souls fall into is something Denise DT, a gifted Money Mindset Coach, calls *procrasti-learning*. Rather than sharing what you know now to avoid the discomfort of being visible, procrastination can set in through seeking to gain more knowledge first. If you find yourself thinking, *I need another certification*, and if this is a pattern for you, I lovingly challenge you to pause. Ongoing learning is beautiful, but your life has likely already equipped you with valuable wisdom. The world doesn't need a more certified you—it needs a more centered and *expressed* you, especially when it comes to mining up your unique wisdom.

I remember when a highly successful friend commanded that I stop hiding behind certifications. On the heels of a spiritual psychology masters program, I had just come back from a few months in India for an extensive yoga teacher certification and was about to enroll in another course. He said, "Use what you already have. Go out there and share it. Charge for it. Otherwise, you'll keep procrastinating the life you imagine for yourself where you're making an impact and generating income sharing what you know. If you want to take another course after that, great! For now, teach what you know and charge for it!"

That moment was pivotal for me. Maybe this is your moment.

Why Storytelling Works to Move Others with Your Message

For thousands of years, we've circled around sacred fires and learned life lessons through stories. Why? Because while facts fade, stories *stick*. They spark emotion, ignite memory, and activate learning.

With each word, a symphony of mirror neurons, oxytocin, and dopamine weaves connection, memory, and emotion into something unforgettable—an invisible thread stitching souls together through story. When you tell a story, especially a transformational one, the listener's brain starts to mirror yours. That's science—and a superpower you can start using today to discover yourself more deeply and bring something beautiful and valuable into our world. **Expertise doesn't come from knowing everything. It comes from *living through something*, overcoming it, and extracting the wisdom.**

Love note: Only share from your scars, not your wounds. When we share what we've healed through, it's empowering.

If it's still raw, give it time. Protect your own heart and give yourself the dignity of your own healing process.

The Value of Your Soul Signature Story

Your Soul Signature Story is the term I use for the origin story of your body of work—the emotional root of why you do what you do. It brings you to life when you tell it. My Soul Signature Story behind my first book, *The Diamond Process™: Using Everyday Triggers to Awaken the Treasure Within* illustrates a time in my life when everything was seemingly perfect externally, but internally I was depressed and romanticizing suicide. I left my life in Los Angeles behind, including the love of my life, and moved to the redwood forest alone to face myself. The healing and transformation I underwent using a seven-step process born out of sheer necessity to heal myself later became an online course, a book, and a coach training certification program. My *why* was to help others who were feeling lost, anxious, or emotionally unstable to gain tools and practices that work so they can embody their authentic selves and establish unshakable inner peace and confidence.

Your Soul Signature Story grounds you during tough moments—when feedback stings, when numbers are low, or when fear creeps in. When your *why* is clear, you don't give up. You keep going because you're serving something greater than vanity metrics. I have an entire module devoted to unearthing your Soul Signature Story in Confident Course Creation School™ because it's that important when it comes to owning your expertise and birthing your body of work.

Your Soul Signature Story also has the power to transform your life through the sheer act of writing it. I've witnessed many women in my membership have quantum leaps in confidence and freedom, and a fierce rise in a sense of purpose through our authenticity circles. I never expected this to happen when I casually suggested we start using some of our Spotlight Coaching Q&A time to share and get feedback on their Soul Signature stories. Woman after woman had a seemingly miraculous *glow-up* like the flip of a light switch. Deanna Turner, a talented professional coach, is a perfect example of this. Here are her words.

"My biggest breakthrough has been completing my Soul Signature Story. This journey has been profoundly healing—it freed me from the weight of painful childhood memories and lifted me from a place of shame to a place of deep love and acceptance for the little girl in my story.

"This breakthrough has not only strengthened my passion for helping women like me, but it has also released hundreds of powerful memories that can now be woven into stories of healing and hope. Most importantly, it has fueled a renewed commitment to the universe—to use my voice and my business as a force for spreading good news, uplifting others, and shining a light on what's possible.

"Thank you for the amazing work you do, Veronica. It's so needed!"

Ready? It's your turn to have your own transformational storytelling breakthrough …

For starters, ask yourself: Why do I want to help others?

Now ask: And why is *that* important to me?

Keep digging until you hit gold.

Let's look at an example. Juliana Spicoluk, founder of Boho Beautiful, seems polished and peaceful on the surface. But behind her success is a story of overcoming great suffering. As a gymnast with scoliosis, she experienced serious back pain, found yoga, healed, and devoted her life to helping others do the same. *That's* her Soul Signature Story.

The Ten Steps of Transformational Storytelling

Let's walk through a framework that helps you take the first bold step in uncovering your Soul Signature Story and communicating it with clarity and power. I suggest putting pen to paper—handwriting has a quiet magic that grounds your energy and invites your creativity to flow more freely. When you write by hand, you slow down enough to hear yourself more clearly.

1. Choose a defining moment

Pick a specific moment that changed you or your perspective.

Example: I was hired to film top-level executive coaches sharing their wisdom for a YouTube channel I created for a consulting firm—but nearly all of the coaches froze on camera.

2. Identify the lesson

What did you learn?

Example: Many empathic leaders are brilliant—until a camera turns on. Visibility fear is real. If it was holding these skilled, successful coaches back, countless wisdom keepers are fearfully hiding out, withholding tremendous wisdom from ever seeing the light of day and positively changing our world. With a few simple energetic practices, sensitive leaders can step into confident visibility almost instantly.

3. Know who this helps

Who benefits from this story? Be specific. (Not *everyone*.)

Example: Coaches, healers, empath entrepreneurs, and creatives who fear visibility.

4. Use a story arc (Setup → Conflict → Resolution)

Setup: Set the stage. Characters, goal, and challenge.

Conflict: Introduce the tension, roadblock, or crisis.

Resolution: Reveal what you did to overcome it. This is the lesson you now teach. This is your expertise.

Example:

- Setup: I was hired to film executive coaches for a consulting firm's new YouTube channel.
- Conflict: As soon as each coach sat on set to film their segment, they fell into fear and panic.
- Resolution: I used three visibility-block clearing techniques to help them recenter their energy and voice their messages with confidence.

5. Clarify who it helps and why

Why should your audience care? Why does this matter to them?

Example: Coaches, healers, and empath entrepreneurs can help exponentially more people and grow their businesses when they know how to clear their visibility fears and confidently voice their messages and make paid offers.

6. Be specific

Use sensory details to bring your story to life. Don't summarize—*immerse*.

Example: Her palms were so sweaty they soaked my hands as I reached out to comfort her before pressing RECORD.

7. Add more sensory details

What did you see, hear, feel, taste, or smell? These details make your story memorable.

Example: As each coach entered. I kept the filming light off and sat them down on the velvet forest green chair and poured a refreshing glass of cucumber lemon water. Before filming, we hummed and took slow, deep breaths to relax the nervous system, get present, and relieve any performative stress.

8. Distill the main teaching point

Toward the end of your story, very clearly state a valuable realization, lesson, or shift in perspective you had. This perspective shift should always be of benefit to the listener, whether it's a helpful way of looking at things or a practice that worked to get a certain result. You can start the sentence with *That's when I realized …*

Example: That's when I realized all it takes is a shift in focus from spinning in an overactive mind to getting actively present in your body to instantly feel confident on camera.

9. Outline the story

Break your story into clear bullet points. Use notecards if it helps you stay organized.

Example:

- If you're a coach or an empath who fears being on camera, I have three energetic tools you can use to confidently voice your message that moves others
- Story of being hired to film executive coaches

- #1 fear nearly every coach had during filming
- That's when I realized all it takes is a shift in focus to instantly feel confident on camera.
- Three tools I used to help them go from self-conscious to self-assured
- Recap three tools and ask which tool would help them the most
- Invite them to practice one of the tools before filming a video and celebrate

10. Practice sharing your story

You've done the preparation work—now it's time to set your valuable voice free. Practice telling your story out loud, to as many different people as you can. Notice when hearts lean in or drift away, and refine with curiosity, not judgment. Each time you share, your clarity sharpens, your confidence blooms. Whether in a safe space like my membership or out in the wild of the world, your story deserves to be spoken. Let it be imperfect. Let it be alive.

Then, when you're ready—or even if you're trembling—take up space. Share your story publicly, not for applause, but as a devotion to your own becoming. Your lived wisdom is powerful. Use the 5 A's to keep your nervous system steady, and remember: Your win is not in being flawless. It's in being brave. Not in perfection, but in courage.

Today's Video Diary Prompt

Take a few moments today to record a short video diary answering the following:

What is one story from your life that taught you something important—something you feel could help someone else?

Speak from the heart.

Trade pressure for pleasure. Enjoy exploring the art of storytelling.

Let this be your jumping-off point and polish your story from there.

If you'd like to take it further, I have a gift for you.
Watch *"Using Your Story to Help Others" Workshop.*

Day 25

Feel Empowered Using the Five-Step Confident Message Framework

What's the most important message you want to leave your audience with—and why should they care? Every listener instinctively wants to know one thing: What's in this for me?
—Oprah Winfrey

Many gifted empaths, coaches, and creatives have deep wisdom to share, but because they haven't learned to hone their messages using a directional structure, they can get frustrated, avoid sharing anything at all, or face crickets when they do share. It can be painful, especially when the desire to be visible comes from a deep calling and a knowledge that your wisdom is worth sharing.

Without a framework, a clear intention, and purpose behind your words, you risk blurting out your thoughts and stories aimlessly, which is ineffective and can create instability and self-doubt as a speaker. This is where the Five-Step Confident Message Framework comes into play to structure your stories and express yourself authentically in a format that sets you up to genuinely serve, empower, and help people.

So far, we've discovered how to clear your visibility blocks, become your own safety, own your expertise, and uncover your transformational story. You've also been freeing your voice and becoming visible to yourself using the video diaries.

Up until now, we've been exploring your voice through a more feminine, intuitive lens. In today's lesson, we weave in the masculine structure—the grounded container that gives your message clear direction and purposeful momentum. Think of this framework as the riverbanks that hold and shape the flow of an abundant river. Your message is the water—alive, powerful, and full of potential. Without structure and direction, it can flood and scatter. But with clear banks to guide it, your words become a purposeful current—capable of nourishing, inspiring, and carrying others toward meaningful discovery and transformation.

The Five-Step Confident Message Framework allows you to take your expansive, beautiful ideas and translate them into potent, purpose-driven communication—whether you're filming a video, leading a workshop, or writing a post. And the best part? It's so easy to use. Many of my students find this content design skill to be a game changer, giving you your next level of confidence in your leadership. The Five-Step Confident Message Framework helps you turn your treasure trove of big ideas into golden nuggets you can easily communicate in minutes.

Having this content creation system will help you take your big, brilliant ideas that may have felt overwhelming in the past and map them out into a cohesive message that ideal clients, students, and viewers will love and appreciate receiving. You'll be able to slip this framework in your back pocket, easily creating impactful content any time inspiration strikes.

Five-Step Confident Message Framework

Before you press RECORD or step onto the stage, take a moment to ground yourself by reconnecting to the gold within so you can voice your message that moves others. This framework isn't just a tool—it's your creative compass. I use it every time I craft a video, a workshop, or a talk. I hand it to you now with joy in my heart, knowing that the wisdom within you can be shared so much easier once you have this. Let it shape your message so your brilliance flows with purpose, pure joy, and power— inspiring others while being fully and confidently expressed.

I sometimes call this the *Who-What-Why-How Map*. Before you create a piece of content, use these steps to get your big beautiful ideas out of your mind and on to the page.

You can download the Confident Message Framework Worksheet I give clients and students. or use a fresh sheet of paper, writing the first four categories of the framework (WHO/WHAT/WHY/HOW) with space between each one to map your content. To access the special worksheet, you can download it here.

Let's dive in.

Step 1: WHO?

WHO are you speaking to? Focus on *one* person—your soul-aligned client, a beloved friend, or someone you wish to help. Speaking to *everyone* leads to overwhelm. Speaking to one person builds intimacy and clarity. When you think of one person you can genuinely serve, it's directional, confidence-building, and supports you in communicating effectively. Notice the difference when you're talking to a friend. Do you ever get stuck when you're telling them a story or sharing your experience? No, of course not. So, before creating your content, think about WHO you are talking to. I call this speaking to your B.F. (best friend or biggest fan). This ONE energetic pivot will make it so much easier for you to share powerfully and communicate clearly.

Pro tip: Look into the camera lens and imagine speaking to that one person. This releases you from rigid performative tendencies and makes the camera feel like your friend. Instead of getting distracted by looking at yourself in the viewfinder or anxiously looking elsewhere, your audience will feel like you're looking directly into their eyes, creating connection.

Step 2: WHAT?

WHAT problem are you solving? This is about clearly and concisely communicating in the first few seconds what your audience is going to get in this video, lesson, or workshop. Whether it's a video or a workshop, clearly state the transformation or takeaway in the first few seconds. Here's an example:

"In this video, I'm showing you how to reconnect with your valuable voice so you stop second-guessing yourself."

Simple. Powerful. Grounding.

Step 3: WHY?

WHY should they care? This is where story comes in. Share a short personal story, metaphor, case study, or even a compelling stat to illustrate why this message matters. This is your chance to take what we learned in the previous lesson and apply it here in the design of your content. Remember, though, you can tell a simple story in a few sentences. You don't have to share an epic, in-depth story. A short illustration can go a long way, serving as a relevant metaphor or direct example of the point you're making.

Anchor your story with this phrase: *The reason I'm sharing this with you is …*

This one sentence highlights the main point so your wisdom lands.

Step 4: HOW?

HOW can your audience apply this? Give them something to do—a journal prompt, an exercise, a tool. Action turns insight into embodiment.

Examples:

- Create a voice memo today expressing your raw truth.
- Use the mirror to practice saying what you *really* want to say.
- Journal: What have I been afraid to say that is now ready to be spoken?

Step 5: REMEMBER YOUR EVOLUTIONARY WHY

Your Evolutionary Why is your soul's reason for showing up—beyond metrics, likes, or validation.

Maybe your why is:

"Because each time I speak, I reclaim myself."

"Because this message is how I free my lineage."

"Because I grow every time I compassionately do what scares me."

Let this be enough. Let *you* be your reason.

This is what makes your visibility sacred. It becomes your soul's playground and your portal to healing.

Today's Video Diary Prompt

Make a short video using the five-step framework. Speak into your camera, just for you, and answer:

When did you feel the boldest in your life—and what helped you feel so brave?

Simplest Plan to Confidently Setting Your Message Free

The more scared we are of a work or calling,
the more sure we can be that we have to do it.
—Steven Pressfield

We've just arrived at a meaningful juncture on our journey together. You've identified your visibility blocks, you've discovered how to clear them, and in the previous two chapters you learned the structure to create valuable content that entertains (using your story) and educates (using your teachings and tools). As you move forward, visibility won't just bring your brilliance forward—it will most likely stir up old fear patterns, too. Celebrate this! Run toward the dance floor. Uncork the kombucha!

Self-doubt isn't a sign to stop. It's a green light saying *GO!* It's a clear indicator that you're moving beyond the familiar zone of ego and into the domain of your soul. Being flooded by fearful, doubtful thinking is feedback that the ego is trying to pull you back into the Vow of Smallness because it's currently unfamiliar with the larger life that your soul is calling you to. And anything that the ego doesn't know, it deems as dangerous and therefore something to avoid.

Having fear or self-doubt is not a sign you're doing visibility wrong—it's a party invitation welcoming you as the guest of honor into your own expansion and embodied confidence. The limiting beliefs and protective patterns that once kept you hidden are rising up because they're ready to be released. They're coming up to come out. Necessary parts of you that you diligently hid behind a mask in order to survive or gain acceptance are also coming up to be integrated so that you can shine even brighter.

To truly liberate your voice and embody confident visibility, you must practice *being* a loving, stable presence for yourself—especially when every part of you wants to run, shrink, or overthink. You get to stay open when you want to close. Feel when you want to analyze. Be present when you want to disappear. The feeling you've been running from is like an orphaned child standing at your door in tattered clothes and with a dirt-smudged face saying, "Please let me in. Please love and accept me." Your ego's reaction might be disgust, but your heart knows exactly what to do. Mother that child into safety and feel the fulfillment of helping them live their full potential. This is what the fears and insecurities that come up through being visible are asking of you—to be held and healed.

Before you commit to sharing your message and being seen, it's important you know fears will come up. This is good news—fertile ground to free yourself.

Expect Hiding Patterns to Resurface When You're More Visible

Perfectionism? Comparison? The Busy Bee Block? The Not Enough Trance? The fear of being misunderstood or persecuted?

Expecting visibility blocks to resurface gives you power. Naming them brings calm and compassion. And practicing your safety tools—like the 5 A's—gives you the nervous-system regulation to meet those moments with strength and softness.

Remember: The win isn't in getting it perfect. The win is *doing it anyway*—and being your own safety in the process.

Your Next Chapter Begins Now

Everything you've explored over our almost 28 days together is not the end—it's the foundation for your next evolution. You're ready to move from learning to *living* the work now.

The key? Consistent, aligned action while being your own safety.

Visibility becomes your daily devotion. Confidence grows as you show up—even when it's messy. Especially when it's messy.

Your 13-Week Devotion: Setting Your Message Free

Now that you have an energetic foundation, some clarity on your expertise, and the tools to support you in becoming your own safety as you're visible, it's time to commit to sharing your valuable voice. Remember, transformation comes from committing to your visibility and being your own safety at the same time. Both are needed to embody confident visibility. The good news is that there's a simple plan that I've seen countless clients and students use that 100% works to help you voice your message that moves others … with confidence!

For the next 13 weeks—one full season of your year—I encourage you to commit to creating and sharing one piece of content each week using the Setting Your Message Free Blueprint, which you're about to discover, and the Five-Step Framework we've already covered in the previous chapter. Let it be playful. Let it be imperfect. Let it be real. In my mentorship community for empaths, coaches, and creatives, we hold each other as we do our good work in the world. It truly is a devotional practice, a way of being a disciple to your dream—to your heart's calling!

Each piece—video, audio, written post, or live talk—is a chance to practice your message, clear your blocks, and own your magic.

What is the Setting Your Message Free Blueprint?

It's simple. Once a week for 13 weeks:

1. **Envision the one person you're speaking to.**
   Anchor in by taking a deep breath and picturing your favorite client, friend, or someone struggling with the problem you enjoy solving.

2. **Start with clarity or curiosity.**
   Open with a single sentence, or what I call a Compassionate Hook. This lets your viewer know if the content you're about to provide is for them or not.

Example: If you've been struggling with _____ and want _____, this video is for you.

Alternatively, you can start with a sentence that sparks curiosity in the viewer, using a statistic or a quote.

Example: Did you know that 80–82% of people feel they have a book in them, yet fewer than 1% ever finish one? Today, I'm sharing the #1 key that the 1% who finish use to become authors.

Another effective way to start your content is with a candid, relatable statement about your own life.

Example: For years, I struggled with anxiety until I made five changes I'm sharing in this video.

3. Tell a story.

Let them feel why this matters through your lived experience, a case study, or an inspiring story.

4. Offer value.

Share a tool, prompt, or guidance they can apply to get the result you demonstrated in the story you told.

5. Celebrate yourself.

Own your courage. Remember your Evolutionary Why. Just doing it is success.

13 Weeks to Confidently Voicing Your Message That Moves Others

Repeat this rhythm for 13 weeks and watch your clarity, confidence, and resonance expand like sunlight cracking through the dawn and into the full glory of morning. The real transformation is going to happen when you show up on weeks that you want to quit. Resistance is a signal that there's something tender within you that wants your love.

You want a real, lasting confidence upgrade? Commit to 13 weeks of becoming your own safety before and after posting each week. Notice how you feel after 13 weeks. Guaranteed, if you apply the emotional and nervous system regulation tools, as you're visible you will feel more empowered than you did before the 13 weeks. If you know you need support in doing this, I have an entire membership and sisterhood of empaths, coaches, and healers designed to walk with you as you're visible. It's the safest, most beautiful group of souls, and you're invited to join us at TheDiamondProcess.com/membership.

Your Only Job: Keep Showing Up

Even when your voice shakes. Even when one post flops or an old story resurfaces. The magic happens when you *don't quit*. This isn't about chasing likes—it's about embodying your light. Every time you create and share, you're not just growing your message—you're reclaiming yourself.

Remember: To thrive as a Visible Empath, the most important one to show up for is you!

Today's Video Diary Prompt

If I ever feel afraid as I become more visible, here's what I want to remember when fear or old patterns try to rise up ...

Record a short video reflection where you name the patterns you expect to arise—and what you choose instead. Speak to your future self. Let this be a powerful resource you can receive and watch anytime you forget how brave, worthy, and magnificent you are.

Energetics of Confident Visibility

Let what comes come, let what goes go.
—Ramana Maharshi

As a little girl, I naturally knew how to share my voice powerfully. Roller-skating on marble floors down the hallway toward the living room of my childhood home, gyrating my hips to make a bold entrance in my black spandex, leopard print leotard, and sprayed towering bangs while singing to Def Leppard. Imagining a sold-out stadium waiting for me as I belted out the lyrics and danced my obsessively rehearsed dance routine on wheels. I was expansion. Life was miraculous, and I didn't need anything in the future to give me such a feeling. Playing a rockstar in my imaginary world was enough for me. I was living fully expressed in the moment.

When my father remarried unexpectedly and I suddenly had a new mother, I no longer felt safe. This wasn't anyone's fault. As a highly sensitive girl, I was already struggling from my parents' messy divorce and the unpredictability of my emotionally unstable mother. In sheer reaction to the persistent tremor of my nervous system, I learned to people-please, become hypervigilant, walk on eggshells, and fawn over those I feared. No longer imaginative and inner referenced, I'd look to my outer world and how the authority figures in my life were responding to me to determine whether or not I could say what I was saying or do what I was doing.

I was leaking so much energy without even realizing it, which is why I started to hide in my bedroom with the door closed. That was the transitory time from lighthouse to sponge. I lost my felt sense of inner power as I became hypervigilant, which is what changes the empath into an absorber rather than a radiator of energy. I'd cry, write poetry, and express my anguish in letters to my boyfriend. My grandmother would sneak a phone into my room so I could plug it in and call my boyfriend and friends to stay connected. It was a painful time when I was punished a lot for small things. In those years, I falsely learned to believe that I was alone, no one was safe, and I didn't have the right to be free and confident. That continued year after year, decade after decade, even with wonderful people around me, without me even realizing it.

Once I became an entrepreneur running my own coaching business in my thirties, I started to learn about frequency and energetic blocks. At one point, I discovered that my programs repetitively capped at 25 students max no matter how big my email community was or how great my promotional reach was. The final straw was when a program I was teaching on confident visibility launched and 24 women signed up instantly, and then with almost three months of enrollment time remaining, no one else signed up—not one person. This was a blatantly clear energetic block or upper limit. I could see that the lack of safety in my nervous system and my subconscious beliefs were at work, making sure that energetically I was deflecting more students from joining than I was accustomed to. My inner thermostat was set to 24 students … 25 of us total!

I finally realized that it was because of a *people block* that I was only allowing a certain number of women into my classes. If I could connect with each of them and please all of them, then I could do my work safely. But in order to feel safe while serving others, if I were to welcome more students, I'd have to be OK with people getting triggered, not being able to read every single feeling in every student, and tend to them, etc.

I did a healing technique on myself that I use in the Prosperous Visibility Mentorship I lead, which helped me reclaim my energy from those people-pleasing years living in my parents' house. Instead of hiding in my room once my stepmom moved in, I envisioned myself roller-skating in the living room the way I once did. I imagined unabashedly being myself, and even inviting her to dance and roller-skate with me, which she did. It was a wonderful vision. In this soul retrieval, my energy was restored. I could feel the safety of being myself and letting other people have their experience, or respond to me without taking it on.

A few days later in a workshop I was giving in my membership, I noticed a couple of students dropped off simultaneously as I was helping someone clear a visibility block, which was a tender moment for her. I suddenly felt concerned about the women who left the call, worrying about them and what they were thinking of me or the program. Were they going to leave? Did they think the work was no longer valuable? Did they think there was something wrong with me or the way I was facilitating? All of these thoughts that were normally unconscious became conscious, lucid. I could see them so clearly. I could feel my body and energy taking so much energy away from welcoming in more abundance and greater service.

I sat with the feeling after the class, and a freshness swept over me that came in through these words …

So much freedom came to me from this one statement. It was an energetic shift. A commitment to my message and the sacred work rather than being liked or making others comfortable. I felt myself restored to the energetic of a lighthouse rather than a sponge.

People can come, people can go, people can love me, people can judge me, I can have huge numbers of students or tiny, and I'm going to keep being me and serving my message. What a shift of focus! This badass rockstar princess on roller-skates was back online! I felt free and alive again. I felt like me!

The win had nothing to do with having more students and everything to do with the satisfaction of being free from letting other people's judgments, actions, or energy define me. The growing numbers are secondary. The primary win is truly embodying this frequency of confident visibility and feeling the exhilaration and aliveness of being my real self sharing my valuable message.

My prayer is that this book has unlocked the energetics of confidently being the Visible Empath within you so you can do what you came here to do and share your valuable voice. It's been such a joy sharing this transformative journey with you. May you lace up your own set of proverbial roller-skates, take your rightful place in the spotlight, and shine as you devotedly serve your unique message that moves the world!

Today's Video Diary Prompt

What does the most confident and visible version of you want to do or say from here?

Stepping into Your Greatness

*There's nothing enlightened about shrinking so that others
don't feel insecure around you. We were all meant to
shine, as children do. And when we are liberated from
our own fears, our presence automatically liberates others.*
—Marianne Williamson

There's something sacred that happens when we stop dimming, stop shrinking, and allow ourselves to fully embody our greatness.

Earlier in this journey, I shared a story from my childhood—a moment when I was targeted simply for shining too brightly.

I wrote that chapter with compassion for the girl I was then. The one who hadn't yet learned that her light could be seen as a threat. The one who didn't know that by being a bright light, she would trigger others. The one who learned to dim.

Looking back, I don't feel shame or regret for trading my authenticity for belonging or for losing myself in others. As a result, I gleaned important lessons over time, one being a deep sense of compassion for myself and others who just want to feel safe and loved.

But if I could go back, I'd wrap her in my arms and prepare her for what was coming. I'd tell her that none of it was her fault. I'd pick her up from school when she was scared of being jumped for having long, luscious hair, confidently answering the teacher's question in class, or smiling too much. And I'd whisper in her ear:

Your light is not the problem. Their discomfort is not your burden to carry.

That moment didn't just mark the beginning of a visibility wound. It marked the beginning of a reclamation.

This chapter isn't just about latent potential. It's about a soul-deep reckoning with the fear of our own power. A fear that's generational. A fear with history.

So many of my clients come to me with visibility struggles that look like perfectionism, procrastination, overthinking, endlessly tweaking bios, websites, or offers.

But the truth?

Sometimes it's not *inadequacy* that's shutting them down.

It's greatness.

It reminds me of a client of mine, Jane Caroline (Transformational Coach, LivinginMiracles.com).

Jane was a star in high school. Fastest girl on the track; only two boys in the whole school could beat her. She was a champion in the making. Strong, disciplined, powerful.

But instead of being celebrated, she was attacked. Other girls, jealous and triggered by her success, began hitting her ankles with hockey sticks during practice.

A message embedded itself deep in her nervous system: *Shine too bright, and you'll get hurt.*

So Jane dimmed. She started smoking. She sabotaged her performance. Choosing *belonging* over brilliance. Choosing *safety* over staking her claim.

Even in her 60s, that fear was still running the show. Still holding her voice hostage. Only it was showing itself in a less obvious way, convincing her to put others' needs above her purpose.

And I get it.

Because if people can't see you, maybe they can't hurt you, right?

If you stay a little smaller, maybe you'll avoid the side-eyes, the jealousy, the judgment.

But here's the heartbreak:

Every time we choose safety over shining, we abandon ourselves.

We leave behind the little girl who knew—*knew*—she was born to shine, lead, love, and inspire.

We think we're keeping her safe. But really, we're keeping her trapped.

Today, Jane has had a *reclamation* of her own! She's cleared her biggest blocks, created her Soul Signature Course, and is now voicing her message that moves others. After parenting her daughter and caretaking her mother for nearly two decades, pausing her own dreams and purpose, she's now in the spotlight helping women over 50 to find their radiance and live their dream lives.

When we first started working together privately, she had one of her big breakthroughs before our sessions even began. I sent her training videos to prepare her energetically for our work together. One of the requirements was to carve out clear office hours every week and honor that scheduled time as she would a doctor's appointment or an important meeting. Having had no time for herself, nor her purpose, this was life-changing for her and an instant upgrade to her sense of self-worth. From there, she kept having breakthrough after breakthrough.

Jane is a force, no longer dimming her greatness to make others comfortable, but rather helping people live in miracles as a result of being the miracle herself.

So I ask you, gently and clearly: Where have you been holding back your greatness? What has the cost been of dimming your light to stay safe, accepted, or understood?

This is your moment.

To stop shrinking.

To stop self-editing.

To stop apologizing for your power.

Other people's reactions are not your responsibility.

Your responsibility is to be the lighthouse.

To stand tall and let others orient themselves in your glow.

Even if it makes them squint.

Even if it ruffles feathers.

Even if it makes people do a double take.

The majority of empaths are walking around like sponges fearfully soaking up the energy of the world. I wrote this book because we're not here to absorb the energies of others; we're light bringers. We're here to be Visible Empaths. We're here to bring the light during dark times.

Your job is not to leave yourself to love others. Your job is to shine and give others the dignity of their own journey home.

Your light is not a threat.

It's a gift.

Choosing yourself isn't selfish.

It's how you shine.

It's how you model wholeness.

Embodying peace in a conflicted world isn't heartless.

It's living proof of what's possible.

So I ask you:

What would it look like to let her out?

The little girl inside of you—the one who danced boldly, spoke freely, felt deeply.

What if *she* is the medicine the world needs?

What if your visibility becomes someone else's permission?

What if your confidence becomes someone else's courage?

This is not the final chapter.

This is a threshold.

The place where you stop hiding.

The holy instant when you trust the value of your voice.

And being your own safety as you share it.

The moment you choose to step into your greatness.

Today's Video Diary Prompt ☑

If I take my foot off the brake and let myself shine, the first thing my greatness wants to express is …

What Now?

If you're feeling the fire, I encourage you:

Make your first public video.

Start your 13 weeks to confidently voicing your message that moves others now.

Or, if you're already visible, share without shrinking.

Say the thing.

Give the value.

Post the truth.

Set it free.

Set yourself free.

And if you want to be held, witnessed, and supported in your sacred visibility journey, join us inside the Prosperous Visibility Mentorship. This community was built for women like you—bold, brilliant, authentic, ready. It's your safe place to set your valuable voice free and live your soul-centered life and purpose!

Together, we're choosing to lead with love.

We're sisters embodying the light.

We're using our voices to spread the good news—not because we're special or chosen, but because we finally stopped shrinking, silencing, and dimming what was always inside us.

This is not a gift for the few. This is an awakening available to all sensitive female leaders, bighearted souls, and empath entrepreneurs who are ready to rise.

Now is your time to drop the tendency to absorb the pain of the world and be who you came here to be.

This is your time to shine as a beacon of light, as a *Visible Empath,* and voice your message that moves the world.

Take a breath and repeat after me:

And so it is!

Afterword

Final Words from My Heart to Yours

If the only prayer you ever say in your
entire life is thank you, that will suffice.
—Meister Eckhart

I recently asked one of the coaches in my membership a question that keeps echoing in my soul: "What would you say to the version of yourself who was too afraid to be seen before joining the membership?"

She had just shared the most hilarious and humbling story about running—literally running—out of a beautiful event space, still holding her plate of hors d'oeuvres and glass of wine, just to avoid the spontaneous *get on stage and say a few words* moment when she was about to be honored with an award. Her fight-or-flight response didn't hesitate—she fled. Visibility was too much. That was then.

Today, she's coaching, teaching, writing, sharing her voice and her wisdom freely with the world. She's not hiding anymore. When I asked her what she would say to the woman who bolted that night, she paused, and then offered the most beautiful truth: "You are safe. You're safe right now."

I loved seeing how far she'd come and that her answer was sincere. The tender place within her that used to run from the spotlight could rest. She was safe because she has become her own safety. After our membership call, I sat in reflection and asked myself the same question. What would I say to the past me who feared visibility?

I saw her—my younger self in Los Angeles, a struggling actress in her twenties during pilot season, flinging herself at the dream with every ounce of hope, fear, and self-doubt she had. I saw her walking into auditions trying to disappear before even being seen, contorting herself into what she thought they wanted, then walking out disappointed, ashamed, and self-loathing. I remembered her standing on stage, doing live theater, and blacking out—not physically, but mentally, disassociating from the fear, from the pressure, from the feeling of not being enough.

And I finally knew what to say to her, so I did. Pressing my hands to my heart and belly, I spoke softly, almost whispering through time to my past self.

Thank you.

Thank you for your courage.

Thank you for not giving up, even when everything told you to.

Thank you for pouring your time, energy, money, and soul into your craft, your calling, your dream.

Thank you for believing in the joy of creativity even when the results weren't there.

Thank you for being the disciple of your dream.

Because of you, I now live a life that once seemed impossible. I live by the beach in a dreamy country, supported by a thriving business filled with the most beautiful souls I get to serve. I have joy, wholeness, confidence, sovereignty. Because of you, I'm thriving.

You didn't fail. You cleared the path. You walked the fire. You did holy work. You let it all burn until all that was left was the one thing that cannot burn. The truth. The radiance. The magnificence. The diamond. And that, dear girl, makes you the greatest success of all.

And to you, reading this now, I ask: Is there a version of yourself you need to thank today?

Don't wait as long as I did.

Don't wait until the success comes or the fear leaves.

Put your hand on your heart now.

Say *thank you* to the part of you that keeps trying, keeps believing, keeps showing up even in the wobble, the fear, the imperfection.

You are not broken. You are birthing.

We're in rapid evolutionary times, and the world needs sensitive, empathetic, light-bringing people more than ever— people like you—to step forward. To demonstrate how we can build and lead from the heart. That tug you feel? That persistent ache to shine? You're being summoned. The time isn't coming—it's now.

This really is your time.

So here is your call to action:

Be a disciple of your dream.

Be kind to yourself. Shine. Speak. Stand tall.

Do the sacred work of being your full self.

If this message spoke to you deeply and you're ready to feel supported in owning your voice, claiming your visibility, and sharing your gifts with confidence, I warmly invite you to join us inside the membership—a heart-centered space for sensitive female leaders, coaches, creatives, and empath entrepreneurs.

As a special thank-you for reading this book, you can join us for a special limited-time offer giving you 10% off using the code: BOOKLOVE

Your voice is meant to be heard.

Your light is meant to shine.

And you don't have to do it alone anymore.

One hand on your heart, one hand on your belly.

Breathe. Repeat after me:

My voice is valuable.
My message is medicine.
This is my time to be the lighthouse I came here to be!

Thank you for joining me in being a Visible Empath, for choosing to voice your message that moves others.

Together, imagine what's possible. Maybe, just maybe, we can move the world!

With all my heart, thank you and congratulations!
Love,
Veronica

Continue the Journey

I'm so grateful you've walked through these pages with me. This book is just the beginning—the real magic happens when you bring these practices into your daily life and connect with a community of like-hearted souls. Below are resources, practices, and ways to stay connected so you feel deeply supported as you continue to shine your light.

✧ Stay Connected

Website: veronicakrestow.com
YouTube: youtube.com/@VeronicaKrestow22
Instagram: @loveronica22

✧ Free Gift for You

The Five A's Audio Practice (free gift) – A guided meditation to balance your emotions and regulate your nervous system so you can confidently share your valuable voice: The DiamondProcess.com/regulate

✧ Want to Go Deeper?

Thrive as a Visible Empath – Join our membership and private coaching community for ongoing support, teachings, and connection as you clear your visibility blocks in a safe space & confidently share your message.

Use code BOOKLOVE for 10% off your membership:

TheDiamondProcess.com/membership (limited-time offer)

Acknowledgments

THANK YOU to R. R. Lowinger for making dreams real. This book was born thanks to you.

To my sister, Kim Sinclair—thank you for being a pillar of love in my life since the day I was born. And for helping me clarify the unique work I do in language people understand.

To the lighthouse women in my membership community— your courage, vulnerability, and soul-centered leadership make our world better. Thank you for trusting me to hold space for your visibility fears and breakthroughs. Who you are in the world has been a driving force behind this book. You are living proof of what's possible for visible empaths globally.

To my soul sisters—especially Jeanne, Shirly, Astrid, and Caroline—your encouragement, support, and celebration throughout this creative journey have worked like magic.

To every client and student who has ever trusted me with your most vulnerable and honest moments—thank you. I learn so much from witnessing you and your truth.

To my YouTube family—thank you for giving me a safe and loving space to share my heart so openly through the years. You have taught me that it's safe to be raw and real while sharing my gifts as a Visible Empath.

To Bethany Kelly at Publishing Partner—you are a godsend! Thank you for gracefully holding me to the fire and walking beside me every step of the way to bring this book into being.

To Jason Frahm—thank you for co-creating the Confident and Visible Empath online retreats with me, which was a catalyst for this book. The transformation we witnessed in thousands of empaths globally planted the seed that now blossoms on these pages. And by heavens, thank you for helping me thrive as an empath and giving me the mantra of all mantras, "not my yobbb!"

To my mother, Verena, you are the epitome of grace. Thank you for nudging me on stage at such a young age, which, in hindsight, was the beginning of this body of work.

To my father, Victor—thank you for believing in me and reminding me that I wrote my first book at six years old and haven't stopped writing since. You are a lighthouse in my life, and your example of what it means to *be the good news* continues to guide me.

And finally ... THANK YOU to the growing number of empaths around the world who are devoted to spiritual growth and being light bringers during these times. Your self-transformation is a bold and beautiful contribution to our human family.

About the Author

Veronica Krestow is a Transformational Teacher, Coach, and Author of *The Diamond Process™: Using Everyday Triggers to Awaken the Treasure Within*—a seven-step system that has served thousands of clients and students worldwide. With a background in professional theater and twenty years of experience as a life coach, Veronica brings a unique blend of artistry, empathy, and soul-centered strategy to her work.

As a Transformational Teacher and Visibility Coach, Veronica empowers empath entrepreneurs, coaches, and creatives to overcome visibility blocks and confidently share their unique messages with the world. Her mission is to help heart-centered leaders transform self-doubt into self-trust—raising consciousness and catalyzing global evolution through the collective of their authentic voices.

Her transformational YouTube channel has received over two million views, and her courses and retreats have impacted audiences across the globe. Veronica's personal journey—from growing up in a materially driven culture in Miami Beach to walking away from a thriving life in Los Angeles to find herself and start her soul-searching path in the redwood forest—infuses her work with grounded wisdom and authenticity.

Now living in Portugal and basking in the sea and sunshine of the Algarve Coast, Veronica embodies the freedom-based lifestyle that becomes possible when empaths and visionaries courageously step into visibility. Through her teachings, she helps others awaken what she calls "The Diamond Self," inspiring a new wave of conscious, confident leaders rooted in love and presence.

The Visible Empath is both a guide and an invitation to that very life.